The Chinese
Information War

The Chinese Information War

Espionage, Cyberwar, Communications Control and Related Threats to United States Interests

DENNIS F. POINDEXTER

McFarland & Company, Inc., Publishers
Jefferson, North Carolina, and London

LIBRARY OF CONGRESS CATALOGUING-IN-PUBLICATION DATA

Poindexter, Dennis F., 1945–
    The Chinese information war : espionage, cyberwar,
communications control and related threats to United States
interests / Dennis F. Poindexter.
        p.   cm.
    Includes bibliographical references and index.

    ISBN 978-0-7864-7271-0
    softcover : acid free paper ∞

    1. Information warfare — United States.   2. Information
warfare — China.   3. Computer security — United States.
4. Computers — Access control — United States.   5. Information
technology — Government policy — China.   6. National
security — United States.   7. Espionage, Chinese.   8. Corporate
culture — China.   9. China — Relations — United States.
10.   United States — Relations — China.   I. Title.
U163.P587 2013
355.4—dc23   2013008761

BRITISH LIBRARY CATALOGUING DATA ARE AVAILABLE

Cover images © 2013 iStockphoto/Thinkstock

Manufactured in the United States of America

McFarland & Company, Inc., Publishers
  Box 611, Jefferson, North Carolina 28640
    www.mcfarlandpub.com

Table of Contents

Preface

This book is about a war that many will doubt we have, an information war with China. To understand it is to believe we do not have war anymore, at least in the traditional sense of it. The new type of war is China's bending a country's will to its own. It is clever, broadly applied, successful and aimed directly at the United States.

The 1990s were the years of Information Warfare, at least judging by the two-inch thick treatise *Information Warfare, Legal, Regulatory and Organizational Considerations for Assurance*, published by the Joint Staff of the Pentagon in 1996, but it was being talked about long before it became fashionable. I think the Chinese were following the strategies before that, but may have been encouraged by our concentration on it. They have applied themselves to it, and have done well for themselves.

This war is neither conventional nor accidental. The U.S. military expanded the doctrine and made it public, but seldom used it themselves. Our military is at a disadvantage in its application because it is part of a system of government that is democratic, decentralized, and separates the government from commercial business. This is a system that has served us well, but it is not one that China sees as a path to the top of the world's food chain.

This is not a "how to" book of strategies that might be developed to fight a war. It is a way to organize what the Chinese are already doing, to make sense of it. Until we see ourselves in a war, we cannot begin to fight it effectively. It doesn't fit our idea of war, because the Chinese have changed the nature of war to carry it out. The First Principle of War is never to be at war with anyone. This is the Escher drawing of war—a stairway that never goes where it should. They will never admit that what they are doing could be interpreted as war. Denial of being at war is part of this form of war.

1

We tend to think of war as something fought by the military, when we know the militaries of the world are often augmented by other types of covert actions, usually carried out by the intelligence communities of different countries. We know that a military attack force can have ground troops who are not in uniform and not working for a military commander. There are helicopters overhead that are "different" from some of the others and are not manned by pilots working for a military. There are support functions that give maps and warnings to attacking military forces. Some of the forces operate from front companies that look like legitimate businesses but are really covered operations. The Chinese use their companies as covers for their government and military, but they are not the only country that operates them. If we don't see them for what they are, they are doing their operational security the way it is supposed to be done. Information war should be below the enemy's radar.

The gap in this book is an area of Information Warfare that is called "black" and involves classified national security information, which is not supposed to be written about in public media. The irony, of course, is that people do actually write about things that are black, and the government even approves some of the things that are said. This is part of a paradox of secrets. We talk about things we do in war, yet we hold these things to be among our most valued secrets.

In this book I've done the best I can to describe some of the aspects of this type of warfare without discussing things that could be related to United States military or intelligence community capabilities. Sometimes that means being vague about what the U.S. might be able to do, or how an enemy might be able to develop other capabilities. Where possible, I have used open sources and what hackers are doing, even though those groups may or may not be sponsored by a government agency. Hackers have caught up to what the governments were doing ten years ago, and the concern today is that terrorists will do the same. It is probably inevitable that it will happen, and when it does, there is almost no deterrent that will stop a stateless group from causing us damage that will be painful. I have tried not to encourage them or point them in any particular direction. Too many people speculate on how to hurt us, without thinking about how that might benefit someone who hasn't thought about the subject very much.

I wrote this book for a general audience and not just for military people. The military does not pay much attention to doctrine unless it serves some interest other than winning wars. This is not a war that the military would fight alone. My purpose is to educate by attempting to teach concepts, not techniques, of warfare. If my audience believes we might already be at war with China, it is a success.

Over the past few years, the Chinese have been doing quite a bit of writing in Information Warfare, not something expected from them. Their doctrine of war is not often public, though they may occasionally offer it for effect. This includes *Unrestricted Warfare* by Liang Qiao, Al Sanbi, and Xiangusui Wang (from a CIA translation of original Chinese text, 2002), and *War Without Smoke* by Ben She (January 2011, offered only in Chinese at present).

Of course many U.S. sources are available in a similar vein. With some notable exceptions, these are generally about Information War in a general sense, and not specific to the U.S. or China. These include:

• Toshi Yoshihara, *Chinese Information Warfare: A Phantom Menace or Emerging Threat?* (Carlisle, PA: Strategic Studies Institute, U.S. Army War College, 2001).
• James C. Mulvenon, *The People's Liberation Army in the Information Age*, Volume 145 (Center for Asia-Pacific Policy and the United States Air Force, National Security Research Division, Project Air Force, RAND, 1999.
• John Arquilla and David Ronfeldt, *Networks and Netwars: The Future of Terror, Crime, and Militancy*, Issue 1362 (Santa Monica: RAND, 2001).
• Zalmay M. Khalilzad and John P. White, eds., *The Changing Role of Information in Warfare* (Santa Monica: RAND, 1999).
• Winn Schwartau, *Information Warfare* (New York: Thunder's Mouth Press, 1995), which I use the example of in the text.
• Daniel Ventre, *Information Warfare* (Hoboken, NJ: Wiley, 2010). This is the most current and the best departure from pure military doctrine. Ventre's contention is that the Chinese focus is on energy and the control of energy, which, while accurate, is not as broad as I have taken it here.

There are several Congressional reports that are very authoritative and well written and, for the most part, I have used these in my sources. They are the only unclassified sources for some of this material. The U.S.–China Economic and Security Review Commission has provided the best sources of any committee of Congress and has done so more frequently than most others. They are both authoritative and thorough.

I have said what I think China has been doing, without mentioning some of the U.S. capabilities to counterattack. Even if the U.S. and its allies were extremely good at Information War, which I don't believe, that doesn't mean this is any less serious a matter. We are behind the Chinese in areas that are going to cause us great harm if we don't start catching up. But it is not something you will hear discussed in the halls of Congress or the Pentagon. These are some of our best kept secrets, and they need to stay that way. We have to learn to fight in similar ways, and we have to do it quietly. Some wars are better fought in the dark.

This book could not have been written without the support and inspiration of my wife, Virginia. A special thanks to Dori Lu Strater, an author and friend who provided some pokes in the ribs to keep this going.

Introduction

To throw by strategic movements the mass of an army, successfully, upon the decisive points of a theater of war, and also
upon the communications of the enemy, as much as possible,
without compromising one's own.
                              — Major General A. H. Jomini,
                              The Art of War, Paris, 1838

This is war, the missile-throwing, bunker-busting, people-mangling
type of war that we think of when we say the word. It is the *Modern
Warfare 3* kind of battle that makes our hearts pound and overwhelms
the senses of adults. General Jomini, one of Napoleon's officers, thought
the first principle of war was to throw the mass of the army on a military
objective, especially communications. The good general may have been
listening to his boss, or talking to Carl Von Clausewitz, who later wrote
On War, known to millions of historians and military commanders. He
said, "We shall not enter into any of the abstruse definitions of War used
by publicists. We shall keep to the element of the thing itself, to a duel....
War is an act of violence to compel the enemy to fulfill our will."[1] War
was fairly easy to figure out in those days, because soldiers lined up with
guns and marched towards each other to throw themselves on "decisive
points" of the battlefield. Those days are gone.

In October 2011, the president of the U.S. sent 100 troops to Uganda,[2]
which seems odd to anyone who heard about it. It seems impossible that
we could be fighting with anyone there, but we are not at war and they
are just advisors, a word I remember well from Viet Nam. It is not war.
The North Koreans exchanged artillery fire with South Korea and that
was not war. In 1982, Britain and Argentina fought battles over the Falk-
land Islands that killed over 800 soldiers and sailors over three months.
It certainly looked like a war, and it may not be over yet. Afghanistan
has lasted 80 years, between the British, Russians and NATO trying to

settle the place. The Afghans seem to be making a living fighting wars but they are not at war with anyone. At least for the last half century, we seem to have run out of wars, even ones where the two sides line up with guns and start shooting at each other. We don't call it war anymore.

I mention this only because the Chinese have stopped playing this game and picked up another that better suits their style. The Americans, British and Canadians gave this type of war a name, but don't play it quite as well. The Chinese are good at Information War. To get to where they are, they have changed the nature of war.

Information War

The Chinese have a concept of People's War, which is a kind of combining of the military, civil government, and business into one strategy for war. Some of it is like our War on Drugs, which is not really a war at all, but is just focusing on a subject to draw attention to it. Some of it is more like real war, but without the killing that usually goes with it. Sometimes, it is real war like we think of it — at its worst. They manage to combine their strategy into goals that can be carried out by the different elements of government. Those goals come out as a five-year plan, a murky document of generalities that says nothing of a war. Nothing about any of this would lead a person to conclude that China was at war with us.

They manage their economy; they develop their military; they mix business interests of the army and commercial business together. Sometimes we forget they can do this because they are a centrally managed, Communist government. That is the Karl Marx kind of Communist government. We don't seem to mind that they are Communist when we buy things from them, but we should probably think about it. They are not our best friends in the world. That, too, doesn't mean they are really at war with us.

They look at the Internet differently than we do. They are careful to control it, while most of the rest of the world does not. We want to be "free" without knowing very much about what that is. A defector told me once that he could tell the difference between a person who was free and one who wasn't. "They act free," he said. I had no idea what he really meant, but it was important enough at the time that he, at the age of 14, left his home and ventured across a barbed wire fence and a minefield. There has to be something strong in a person to do that. The Russians, Chinese, Syrians, and Iranians know what it means.

To see a blind man find his way to the U.S. Embassy in Beijing; to see him threatened (at least according to his words) and intimidated, while the government says to the U.S., "This is none of your business"; to see the press get pushed around repeatedly by the Chinese Army and Police; to see the State Department roll over and let this fellow go because the Chinese offer him safe passage, is just politics. To see his suffering in that kind of environment is what free means. They are not free, but that does not mean they are at war with us.

Countries we don't always see as free are a growing number of our neighbors on the Internet. North America used to own the Internet, when it came to usage, but not anymore. Since 2000, the Chinese have *added* more people to their Internet user base than are in the United States. Countries like Russia, Iran, India, China, Pakistan and Turkey are not fond of the U.S. and they also have been adding more people proportionate to their populations than we have. Worse, they are not afraid to use the Internet as a vehicle for Information War, their criminal enterprises, and making trouble for the rest of us.

Al-Qaeda puts up a website that tells its sympathizers to start fires in places where the weather is dry and they tell them how to find out the earth is dry. They know that fires are not going to kill a lot of people but they are going to cause disruption in services and cause property damage that, since 9/11, has not been easy for them to do. They will try to take credit for every "natural" fire that occurs for the next few years. This is a terrorist group waging the only kind of war they can. Some people are grateful that they can't do much better, but they don't have trouble seeing this as war. We know we are at war with al-Qaeda. They stick their finger in our eye every chance they get. The Chinese are more subtle.

The Chinese Internet Is Not Our Internet

The Internet has become a medium of war in the same way imagery, like the millions of cell phone pictures, streaming video, and audio recorders have added to our communications capabilities. These are all similar to television in their effect, especially when combined with social media. The Chinese do not allow their people to use the Internet the same way we do. They are developing something called the Golden Shield. China's Golden Shield Project got off the ground in 1999 as part of a larger effort to build up the capabilities of their bureaucrats to keep an eye on almost everyone. In 2000, the Chinese Communist Party Central Committee brought in 300 companies from a dozen or so countries to talk about building a surveillance network that would combine the national, regional and local police and security agencies to monitor every citizen of China. They can match data against the new national ID cards carried by everyone. Communist countries do this sort of thing regularly, but not on this scale. The concept is ugly.

If we took the federal agencies involved in national security, law enforcement, prisons, jails and border patrols, personnel management, traffic management, crime statistics, fugitive warrants, foreign affairs management, combined them with the task forces, state vehicle departments, and regional police, and linked in the local police forces, we might be able to have something close to what they are trying to build. It wouldn't include everything they are trying to get, but it would be close. We don't have an office for population control, as the Chinese do, so we are never going to get there.

The Golden Shield is supposed to construct databases of criminal records, fugitives, stolen vehicles, driver's licenses, migration data and records on every adult in China. With such a system, it is possible to keep pretty close tabs on just about everyone, but surely those who might not be happy with the government, though that may not be its purpose. China would say this is an internal matter of no concern to us.

Privacy advocates, Congress, civil rights groups and a few others would be up in arms if we were to try to extend police cameras to identify Republicans, Scientologists, members of labor unions, people with unpaid parking tickets, parolees, or those who might search for some religious groups on the Internet. If it were just in their own country we would not have much to say about it, but they don't stop there. You will remember that, when the Chinese decided to hack e-mail of dissidents, they started looking at e-mails in the U.S. too. This is all part of the Information War, but it has come upon us slowly and with not much fanfare.

We usually think of war only as something done by the military, but that is a narrow view. In *The Changing Role of Information in Warfare*

(RAND, 1999),[3] we are told that information will make a military stronger by leveraging and synthesizing the capabilities that already exist. That goes for terrorists too, of course. One of the Obama Administration's big concerns is that the tactics we use in the Information war will spill over into the world of terrorism. That kind of concern is too late, but better late than never, in this case.

Seven types of warfare are documented both by RAND and by Defense Department doctrine: economic, command and control, electronic, intelligence-based, psychological, cyber, and hacker war. This is what some people call "total war"— the mixing of combat operations with disruption and control of economic and political functions of government. Not only militaries carry out these kinds of things, but they are generally behind it. We are not very good at it, but the Chinese seem to have been paying attention, even if our militaries were not.

Economic warfare is the manipulation of information exchanged in trade (either denial or exploitation) as an instrument of state policy. We usually don't think of this as war, even though it is. Wars are fought over who gets to trade with whom, and what they get to trade. Trade routes are big targets in a war, and we know that even a hint of trouble in the Gulf of Oman will raise gas prices in the U.S. by a dollar or more. But that is not the kind of thing this is about.

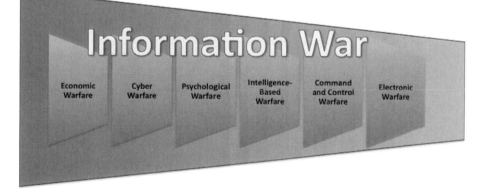

From 1995 to 2000, the Defense Department published a series of policy and operational planning documents that described the basic elements of Information Warfare and how the department should use it to improve its capability to fight.

The Chinese use their intelligence services and military to collect information from the competition and feed that back into their companies. From a policy view, they steal information as a part of their national strategy to win an economic war. Their military owns some companies and what they don't own, the Central Committee controls. They win bids; they control their own commodity prices; they harass the competition as they did with Walmart and Rio Tinto. They steal intellectual property, which they then use to compete with the companies they steal it from. They leverage their surplus for political benefit and manipulate their currency valuation. They call this competition; we call it a few other things, but none of them are war.

Chinese companies are not what our Western world business experience would make of them. They look like our businesses. They have boards; some are privately held. They have articles of incorporation and bylaws, but they are still controlled by the government. Some of them are owned and operated by the People's Liberation Army. We see that difference in public very rarely, but it happened with Alibaba.

Anyone who follows the Internet knows about Alibaba and Yahoo! Alibaba is not some little Silicon Valley start-up. It has 23,000 employees in China, India, Japan, Korea, the U.K. and U.S., getting startup capital from Softbank, Goldman Sachs, and Fidelity. It includes Taobao Marketplace and Taobao Mall, which are the Amazon and e-Bay of China; Alibaba Cloud Computing, which does a cell phone operating system and is building the equivalent of Amazon's Cloud; China Yahoo!; and Alipay, the PayPal of China, which claims to be bigger than PayPal.

In 2011, investment companies were buzzing over Alipay, and for good reason. In the business world as we know it, corporate moves are decided by the board of directors, if a company is public, like Alibaba. Companies that own substantial amounts of stock generally have a say in these moves. There may be a board fight, but at least the board will know what is at stake and what has been proposed. Imagine Yahoo!'s surprise when Alibaba transferred ownership of Alipay to a Chinese company that is owned by the Alibaba Group CEO. They didn't find out about this for seven months.

This would be like Ford transferring the Lincoln division to another company, owned by its CEO, and not telling the stockholders they were going to do it. Alibaba claims it did this because of government regulations, but even that does not get in the way of board actions anywhere else in the world. They would recognize the regulations and discuss what was going to be done with the company. These are not real boards of directors.

Alibaba hired the former general counsel of the U.S. Trade Representative (USTR) to help with Taobao's listing as a "notorious market" by USTR. This just means they sell things that are knock-offs and counterfeits. Taobao is still listed because it "is a site offering a variety of infringing products to consumers and business that while continuing its significant effort to address the problem, reportedly also continues to offer infringed products." Don't you love this kind of language? They hate to hurt each other's feelings.

What it did was wake everyone up to the idea that the Chinese do not do business the way the rest of the world does. Their government can, and will, act to control its business sectors whether the rest of world likes it or not. It put the world on notice, and it was not the kind of thing that went over well in the markets. It makes every agreement to invest, especially in stock, suspect, but the Chinese government controls business interests in how they use the Internet. They will protect their Internet, even if it hurts.

Command and control warfare (C2) to attack the enemy's ability to issue commands and exchange them with field units; these are called, in turn, anti-head and anti-neck operations. Anti-head and anti-neck are ridiculous terms that nobody uses in real life. All this attacking of people in command is not new. Every general who ever lived knew it was a good idea to kill off the other generals and officers who were leading the troops. Now, we can isolate them and cut them off, and it doesn't matter quite so much if they are dead. But, what is different about this is we might even need them alive, if we are issuing orders in their name. We want to isolate them and cut them off, but not kill them.

Early in the 2008 presidential race, the Chinese hacked accounts of the McCain and Obama campaigns, apparently looking for position papers and the direction the candidates would take. This is the kind of *looking around* that identifies who is writing the kind of things the president will read and how they think. They hacked the accounts of congressmen and their staff members. Around the same time, they hacked the account of the secretary of defense. Two members of the House of Representatives, one of them my representative, said they were hacked by Chinese-based computers because of their investigations into human rights violations. Others, whose names do not appear in the press, have been hacked too.

Occasionally, we hear of some hacker attacking a bank or a government agency and we just think of it as another of these gangs of hackers making money. We don't put all of the things that are going on into a common mesh. One of the things making that more difficult is *attribution*. We can't say for sure that any one thing came from China, originated in China, or was supported by the Chinese government. We can't say whether the intent was criminal or intelligence collection. I can steal a list of corporate officers, home addresses, family members, e-mails and telephone numbers, and I could just be trying to make up a mailing list. I could be trying to identify potential extortion targets. I could be developing a list of people I want to replace with people I control so I can take over the company. I could be making a list of people to issue employees' e-mails telling them to not come to work on a day we are launching a side war against Taiwan or Myranmar.

The example of GhostNet makes this easier to understand. About all anyone can authoritatively say about this network was in two reports by the Information Warfare Monitor and Shadowserver Foundation, published a year apart.[4]

In the first report, researchers said they were not so sure that China itself was involved and that the spike in Internet hacking from China could be due to a 1000 percent increase in Chinese users over the last 8 years. In their April 2010 analysis, *Shadows in the Cloud*, they had much more on how information was being stolen, what it was, and where it was going. They started looking at an example. The target was the Dalai Lama. The information being stolen was coming from Indian embassies in Belgium, Serbia, Germany, Italy, Kuwait, the United States, Zimbabwe, and the High Commissions of India in Cyprus and the U.S. Not very many ordinary hackers have an interest in the Dalai Lama.

The control servers for these attacks were in Chongqing, China, and the Chinese are certainly interested in him. The control servers used social networking sites, webmail providers, free service hosting providers, and large companies on the Internet as operating locations and changed them frequently. They used similar, specifically targeted attacks against users, and collected 1500 letters from the Dalai Lama's personal office.

They also sucked out the contents of hundreds of e-mail accounts located in 31 different countries.

The difference in the accountability to China between the two reports was *attribution*, the ability to say with reasonable certainty who was behind the hacking. Suppose Iran was operating those websites, telling people to set firebombs off in the forests of Northern California. The website pretends to be al-Qaeda, but do we really know for sure? That is what natters in attribution — we have to know with reasonable certainty. The same thing is true of war. If someone sinks a cruise ship in the Gulf of Mexico, we would like to know where the attack came from and who was behind it. Everybody will know it sank, but they might not know who did the deed. Before we attack Mexico over this sinking, it might be worth the effort to find out who did it. On the Internet, that can be harder than in the physical world.

Now, can we speculate about how these Dalai Lama e-mails and letters are going to be used? Yes, but it is only a guess. When anyone knows your plans for the next few years, your objectives, your approach to meeting your objectives, and the people who you have identified as those helping you with that success, they have a powerful tool to apply to undoing those plans. It is not what you think of as war, but it depends on whether it is the Dalai Lama or the Chinese government who is looking at it. When a country steals your internal mail, it feels like they are after you. It can seem like war. In the Dalai Lama's case, it might even be war, but war with whom? And, what can he really do about it?

Attribution can put a spotlight on some things that governments would like to keep under the rock of secrecy. The Dalai Lama is not surprised that the Chinese might steal his letters, since they are not on the best of terms. What he would like to know though, is whether it was really China.

Even though there are nearly a billion Internet users, those numbers don't make it impossible to find the people who are trying to get into information systems. Hackers are watched by other hackers, people in governments, and private-sector companies. So, they have to take steps to make sure they don't get caught; or, they cover their tracks so they can deny doing anything wrong. It takes time to find the right people, just as it took time to find out who was responsible for the 9/11 attacks. We didn't launch an attack on Saudi Arabia, even though most of the hijackers were from there. President Bush had to figure out who was really behind it and it took time.

The long process of identifying where and how the attacks on the Dalai Lama came from, brought them to China. This is because investigators talk to each other, telling how one attack or another was done. They started to see the same techniques, from the same locations, being used to attack other systems. There were 760 companies in all, and 20 percent of the Fortune 100. That is a scary number. This is the kind of attack, spread over several months, and extremely successful, that can get our leaders excited and ready to do something. It is right on the dividing line between war and not war, and that is where the Chinese like to stay.

Electronic warfare to enhance, degrade or intercept radio, radar, or cryptography of the enemy. This is an old, very sophisticated, highly classified field that has had more success than most of the other areas of Information War, yet almost nothing is known about how it is done, or where. That is a good thing. Hackers, today, use some of the same techniques and attacks, but few of them know that some of the things they have been doing have been done for a long time. Usually, if a government is doing it, it is classified national security information, and there will not be much to see of it. Generally speaking, if people are talking about it, it isn't the government doing the talking. They like to keep this quiet.

A good example is the Obama Administration's consideration of using viruses to attack the radars of Libya's military.[5] *Wired* reported the Administration considered attacking Libya's radar sites but thought it might take too long to get the plan together and launch it. We don't see much like that in the press ever, and certainly not from any Administration in recent memory. The obvious difference between what the Russians did in Georgia and what the *Wired* article is talking about is the military-on-military aspect of it. No country likes to talk about this kind of thing, and no administration ever should.

Starting in November of 2010, several systems were hacked by someone who established over 300 control systems, almost all around Beijing. What made this different was the attackers were going after a place called RSA that was famous for its ability to do encryption of various sorts. RSA makes a token that many in business have seen. A user logs onto a home network and the software asks the user to type in a long number that is read from the token. It is just that one time, and it changes, so it is not the same number the next time. The nice thing about the RSA token method is you can be pretty sure anyone who logs in with it is an authorized user. We would probably think a place that makes security devices would be secure, but over the past couple of years, more than one of them has been successfully attacked. The people doing it are good.

During the next few months, several other major companies were hacked, only there is a pattern to these that will make anyone nervous who sees the list.[6] There is the IRS, Verisign (another crypto-solutions company), USAA, which primarily handles insurance and banking for military people, several locations of Comcast and Computer Sciences Corporation, a few locations of IBM, the U.S. Cert, which handles investigations into computer incidents at the Federal level, the Defense Department Network Information Center, Facebook, Fannie May, Freddie Mac (just so we have most of those housing loans covered), Kaiser Foundation Health Care System, McAfee, Inc. (the virus people who do nearly all of Defense networks), Motorola, Wells Fargo Bank (and Wachovia, now owned by Wells Fargo), MIT, University of Nebraska–Lincoln, University of Pittsburgh, VMWare, the World Bank, and almost every telecommunications company of any size, anywhere in the world. That last one included all the major telecoms in China. So, they are hacking their own telecoms. It is almost like someone said, "Go out and get everything you can." There are probably some that have yet to be discovered.

Intelligence-based warfare is the integration of sensors, emitters, and processors into a system that integrates reconnaissance, surveillance, target acquisition, and battlefield damage assessment. These techniques can be used to both seek and hide assets. Iran and North Korea have taken to building their sensitive sites underground, which certainly is not new, but is a recognition of how effective other countries have been at discovery of their capabilities. If a country wants to hide what they are doing, it costs them quite a bit in resources to do that.

Psychological warfare is the use of information to affect the perceptions, intentions, and orientations of others. Psychological warfare is probably the oldest and best-known form of Information War. Think Tokyo Rose and her radio broadcasts to GIs in World War II. When the Chinese lowered the value of their currency after warning us about putting more restrictions on trade, they were making a point that they had the ability to disrupt our economy. They don't have to do anything else for the psychological effect to take hold.

I was kind of surprised to see a picture of a J-20 Stealth Fighter in the *Wall Street Journal*. The *Wall Street Journal* is not known for its aviation reporting, nor digging up important news on stealth fighters in all the different countries of the Asian Pacific. It turns out, the U.S. secretary of defense just happened to be visiting the Chinese that day, and this fighter was sitting out on a runway where anyone could see it. It taxied around a little while to make sure nobody missed it. Lots of pictures were taken, by anyone with a heartbeat, and sent to newspapers and magazines over the earth. How odd.

Since I spent most of my military life protecting weapon systems so they couldn't be seen before they were operational, I know the principle involved here. It takes a lot of money and time to get a stealth fighter to fly. Before anyone in the world sees it, no military force on earth wants another military to know that it exists. They hide it in hangars, fly it at night, or do other things that make it more difficult for people who look for stuff like that to find it. They don't want people to see it until it gets to the point where it can be used for something. That is usually an operational mission where it collects intelligence or bombs something. When other militaries see it, they are going to want to start working on something better, or some way to counter its capabilities. For a few months, maybe a year or two, the advantage is useful to those who have it, but it will eventually be overtaken. It is a kind of game, but a serious one.

We saw the same thing with the Chinese aircraft carrier, the first they had ever set on the water.[7] The BBC called this the "worst kept secret in naval aviation history," and they are only just getting started refitting the thing. The Russians built it and China said it was going to be used as a floating casino. When they got it into port, they started to work on it and it was obvious it was not being equipped as a new casino unless the customers could land on a moving deck. You can't hide an aircraft carrier while it is sailing around on the ocean, but they can hide it while it is being built. They haven't been trying to hide it or even conceal what its real purpose might be. They could have said they were building a test vehicle or a cruise ship, but they didn't even want to do that. This is openness that is curious.

Something similar occurred in 2009.[8] Two months after President

One of the ships from which crewmen dropped wood into the water in front of the USS *Impeccable* operating in international waters, but in seas claimed by China (U.S. Navy).

Obama was sworn in, some Chinese ships intercepted a U.S. ship, the *Impeccable*, which was towing a gadget that looked for submarines. This happened in international waters. The crews of these Chinese ships were throwing wood in the water, fishing around for the line holding the sonar array, and running the ships in the path of the Americans, in a way that was clearly not intended to be friendly. The encounter was unusual enough, but nobody normally does this kind of thing in such a public way. Open seas, clear day, close-up is not the usual way to play this game. It was bizarre.

These are images of what might be a step towards war. It isn't war; it is just a picture of what could happen in war, and it was intended for a number of different audiences that saw it — their own, and others. The Chinese stealth aircraft was one of a kind, but it serves its purpose. They can, and will, maybe build more of them. They might even build more aircraft carriers one day, as BBC speculated, or maybe they will just build one. They want us to guess. *Jane's* published a picture of a cave entrance where Chinese submarines were going into and out of the base of a mountain on the coast. There could be 100 of them in there, or just a couple with the numbers being repainted each time they come and go. It is deception — all part of war. The Internet will allow them to get these images out to large numbers of people and not just to the intelligence services of people who are spying on them.

They could keep quiet about them, and only the intelligence services of the world will know anything much about what they can do. Only they didn't. There is no filtering by the intelligence communities of other countries. They didn't try to hide them and released them at times there were things going on in the world that could be affected by them. In the first case, the visit of the secretary of defense; in the second, the testing of a new president; in the third, a few months after the ASEAN Forum, when the U.S. was invited back into the region. At least for now, they find it more useful to make images of war than make war. They have been doing this for some time.

Cyberwar is the use of information systems against the virtual personas of individuals or groups. This is really attacking people, or groups, as they exist in digital form. It is a little bit like *Avatar*, in a way, except machines can be the same as people, and people can have more than just one avatar. They can live in private networks of war machines, or in the Internet. In a virtual world, a machine can be a person and can function the same way. It is possible to be more than one person at the same time. It can be difficult to find the real you, and that may be what is intended. It is just as easy for someone to be you and act as you might. We seem to get e-mail, advertising Viagra, from some of our best friends. It is somewhat the idea of information war. Cyberwar is usually used in conjunction with one of the other types of Information War, and is the newest form of it, but it should not be confused with hacking for a criminal purpose. It is more sinister than that. Besides the potential to undermine basic military services, people are hacking our banking structure, home loans, electricity grid and lots of other things. But, they are also going one step further. The Chinese are trying to undermine our telecommunications infrastructure by buying into it, and having a substantial market position in equipment, where they cannot.

Most of the world's telecommunications infrastructure is owned by about 50 companies. AT&T is still the largest, by revenue, followed by

Vodaphone in the U.K., Telefónica in Spain, China Mobile, Nippon Telegraph and Telephone, and Verizon. These are all global carriers, so they operate in quite a few countries and have agreements with the other carriers to swap services where they need access. They overlap in some countries, but not all. Every country, for national security reasons, has some limitations on what ownership another country can have in its infrastructure. China enforces theirs, as do we. We all do this in the name of national security.

The Chinese are trying to buy into the U.S. infrastructure using, among others, Huawei, and the U.S. has not been willing to let them do it. In the past two years, Congress and the Committee on Foreign Investment have intervened in Huawei's attempted purchase of 3-Com, 3-Leaf, a piece of Motorola's network infrastructure (later sold to Nokia Seimens) and Emcore, a New Mexico–based company that sold fiber optic equipment. It is clear our government does not intend for them to be successful.

Both Huawei and ZTE, the second largest equipment maker in the world, were excluded from a Sprint/Nextel bid and several U.S. senators were said to have sent a letter encouraging them to be denied that opportunity. They were stopped in similar bids on AT&T networks and 2Wire, a U.S.–based company owned by Pace, a British firm. 2Wires's main business was residential broadband. The Commerce Department recently said that Huawei was not going to be allowed to bid on a contract for a national wireless network for first responders,[9] because they believe Huawei may be linked to the Intelligence Services of China.

At the same time, Motorola brought suit against them for industrial espionage. The suit said several of Motorola's employees conspired to steal Motorola's technology and transfer it to Huawei through a shell company, Lemko, created by one of the employees. That employee sent some of Motorola's proprietary information to Huawei in 2003. When one of them was arrested by the FBI at O'Hare airport in Chicago, she was carrying 1000 Motorola documents and had a one-way ticket to China.[10] The case was settled out of court in 2012. If Huawei is not linked to Chinese intelligence, it is the most persecuted company in the history of international trade.

If they are linked to the intelligence functions, then we might have reason to consider it unfortunate that Huawei has agreements with Vodaphone to supply network equipment. China Unicom and Spanish telecom Telefónica are combining investments that they claim will be 10 percent of the world's market. Unicom gets a seat on the board of directors. Through a separate deal, Telefónica and Vodaphone are sharing infrastructure in Europe, putting Huawei, which has separate deals with both of them, in better position for expansion. Huawei is a supplier to Telefónica to put its equipment in a new technology center in Germany and supply infrastructure and service to Germany, the Czech Republic, Spain and Latin America. They own a large piece of the infrastructure of Nigeria and Pakistan. Huawei has over 600 contracts in Iraq and are said to "own" the national telephone system.[11] It was nice of Iraq to give them those contracts, now that we are pulling out our last troops. These infrastructure deals put China in control of large portions of the world's telecommunications.

Huawei makes equipment, keeps the software in it updated, and supplies patches to those who need them, just as any other manufacturer would. This gives them the capability to shut down any network their government wants, or exploit it for its intelligence value. Huawei may not be doing it, but they are not in a position to stop it either. When Blackberry started having trouble in Europe and the U.S. with their network, I wondered how much of it was operated with Chinese equipment. Blackberry has been a thorn in their side for a long time because their systems are secure. Nobody will ever prove that they were part of that, and that is the advantage they have in controlling large parts of the world's infrastructure. Attribution will be difficult, but everyone will know they have the capability. It gives them an edge.

Last year, for 18 minutes, quite a bit of network traffic was re-routed to China.[12] Most of it was from our Defense Department. Was it an accident? This tickles my imagination because it just doesn't seem like something that happens as an accident might. Since it does happen in various parts of the world, on a regular basis, it is possible. It is also possible it was just a practice for something bigger.

Hackerwar is the use of techniques like bad software to destroy, degrade, exploit, or compromise information systems both military and civilian, such as the Stuxnet Worm and some of its cousins. The worm attacked Iran's ability to make weapons grade uranium in its laboratories by affecting centrifuges made by Siemens. This worm could have come from anywhere, but it was widely attributed to Israel and the

United States. "Widely attributed" is about as good as it gets in this line of work.

Information War is only part of war, but it is a part we can relate to. We rely on information systems to do most of our work and social contact and it looks like the Chinese see that as important to their ability to fight. At the same time they develop their strategies for Information War, they are strengthening their ability to fight real wars by increasing support for space operations, nuclear combat capabilities, and cyberwar.

China had 15 space launches in 2010, a national record, and they have a program to get something on the moon. This is the first year that they equaled the U.S. in launches. They have developed anti-satellite weapons and may have intentions of using them against both communications and spy satellites. They practiced by using one on an old Chinese weather satellite, and the U.S. has accused them of using lasers to blind our satellites.[13] They have just launched their fifth GPS satellite, which can mean a number of things, but mostly that they want their own, rather than using someone else's. They may just want to have some, if they decide to shoot all the others out of the sky.

They have stepped up their espionage. In the past 15 years, China has stolen classified details of every major nuclear and neutron bomb the U.S. had in its inventory.[14] They have had ongoing espionage activity at the nuclear laboratories — Los Alamos, Lawrence Livermore, Oak Ridge, and Sandia — that produce and develop the weapons. This allows them to make their weapons smaller and easier to shoot a long way on a missile.

China has stolen U.S. missile guidance technology and exported it to other countries like Iran, Pakistan, Syria, Libya and North Korea. They sold medium range missiles to Saudi Arabia and they trade extensively with Iran, which is not our best friend after trying to get Mexican drug gangs to hit embassies in Washington, D.C.

We seldom hear much about cyberwar, though there have been accusations that the Russians and Chinese have planted software in our electrical grid that will give them control of it if they want to use it.[15] They have been accused of introducing counterfeit servers and other Internet equipment that appear to belong to legitimate companies but were not made by them.[16] They are probably doing all of these things and quite bit more. Nobody is going to produce proof of it, since it could be right on the verge of war, and it is the kind of war the Chinese could wage, but we could not. Ignoring it will not help make it go away.

Besides chips, the Chinese make quite a few other network components. Several different types of hard disks are made there, including HP, IBM, and Western Digital, some of the most used storage drives in the world. Chinese companies make workstations, PCs, wireless equipment, routers, servers, DVD players and recorders, motherboards, cables, the test equipment we use to test all of these, and 300 anti-virus products. If you want to build a network of computers, you can get all the things needed to do that, and a company that will build it for you. Even if you get another company, it would be hard to avoid buying components that were not made in China. This gives them leverage and potential for controlling large portions of the Internet in war.

Imagine the Stuxnet worm in big numbers, everywhere. Stuxnet is very complicated as a means of war and is certainly not a war that we understand very well. If crippling the centrifuges in Iran is an act of war, then somebody is at war with Iran. We just don't know who it is. Whether such a thing is an act of war is debatable. If Israel admitted they set it free, then Israel and Iran could be at war. That would be complicated and they both would have to admit to being at war. So when this first was being talked about, Israel said it didn't do anything. Iran denied it ever happened. Nobody is at war. This is bizarre, if you think about it long enough.

The Iranians have taken to saying the Stuxnet worm was planted in its systems by the United States. They added this thought when they started stepping up the rhetoric against us after the U.S. and European Union tried sanctions to get the weapons development stopped. The Iranians say that did not work, so we planted the worm. Pick a country with computers and it could fall to any one of the them. The beauty of attribution is it works for everyone on the planet.

What the Chinese have the potential to do is increase Stuxnet by a factor of 1000 or more, and they have the delivery mechanisms already in place. They already make them and can put worms or special codes in almost any thing, waiting for the right time to turn it on. Stuxnet turned out to not be as controllable as it should have been, but in an all-out war, this will not matter very much. As an opening round in any other type of war, it might work pretty well. It can stop communications, or slow them down enough to open up other avenues of attack.

The Chinese would argue that they are a peaceful country, just protecting themselves, but their doctrine would leave many doubts about that. We should judge them on their methods and the results. I spent my career in a Cold War with the Soviets, where we were open about our disagreements and the way they gobbled up territories around them. We knew we were at war. We don't see it quite a clearly with the Chinese just yet, but one day, we will.

1

The First Principle of War

Sometimes we forget what being Communist means. They don't operate the way we do, and they are not free. They are comfortable with that. We grew up in a different kind of neighborhood. A Communist country, as a rule, will control its population more than a democracy can, but they need buffers against the rest of the world to keep a tension on their own people and keep the focus off of themselves. Russia did it with the Eastern European satellites, and when they could no longer control them, it didn't take them long to forget their old loyalties.

The Chinese, in particular, have some really unsavory neighbors, who seem to cause most of trouble in the world. North Korea is number one on that list. They are not free either, but they didn't learn that from the Chinese. The North Koreans are going to fire another missile over the South China Sea, and the last time they did that, the Japanese were not very happy. This time, Japan has a missile defense system that they are thinking about trying out. How would it be if Bermuda decided to shoot down our satellites as they were being launched over the Atlantic? We probably would not like it very much. On the other hand, if it is really a test of a weapon, and not the launch of a satellite, can Japan shoot that down? This makes politics more complicated and allows the Chinese to be observers and not directly involved in that action. It is a way to observe what we will do in war. It is bringing other countries close to war, but not getting close themselves. They are good at it. It is a clever way to push an adversary and see how they will respond, but not be the enemy.

Myanmar might have been free once, but they changed their name from Burma and cut themselves off from the rest of the world, so very few people remember anything about them. In 1988, their military leaders killed 3000 of them in putting down a rebellion and China gave the military more arms. Tibet has not done so well in their dealings with

China, but they don't cause any harm to people around them. A few of the nuns and monks will set themselves on fire to show how they feel about the Chinese, but they are not shooting strangers or having a war that we would understand. It is hard to see setting yourself on fire as anything good, but Tunisia started off that way, last year, and ended up free of its dictator. It is a strange and mysterious kind of war that is difficult for someone of our culture to understand. It is nice to be part of the revolution that might result, but burning to death is not very pleasant to contemplate.

How do we react to this kind of war? We make friends with Myanmar, which offers release of a few political prisoners to cement this relationship, and the nuns and monks continue to set themselves on fire. The Chinese know we are not going fight over Myanmar and we know they are right about that.

Viet Nam has not been one of our best friends over the years, but they are better friends now than when I was in college. We called that the Viet Nam War and we did fight in that one. It was ugly, vicious, and cost us too many lives to justify what we have now. The Chinese know we will fight in some situations, even a long way from our own shores, and in a very unpopular situation. At least, we will do it for a while. They learned how to fight our Army and Marines on the ground and they brought in help to fight our Air Force. China was watching and helping out, as any good neighbor would.

My uncle was in the Korean War, where they would have done the same thing they have done with Viet Nam, but our Army had just fought a war and remembered how. They got some friends from the new United Nations and fought directly with China. Lots of countries in the world have, but it did not work well for anybody who fought there.

Japan fought a war with China before World War II, and neither side likes the other very much because of it. India and China fought a war in 1962, and it seems like we should be able to remember that. India still remembers. Russia and China have fought on their own border, but nobody called that a war except the people who were actually in it. Most people don't even remember that it happened. China is pretty cozy with Iran and Syria and these folks are not exactly close with anyone, but they are not on China's border either. Afghanistan is. So is Pakistan, right on the side where we seem to be having so much trouble with terrorists hiding out.

China is never at war. Its neighbors are. Did you ever notice that?

We assume, at some point, the Chinese will see the light and start doing things the way the rest of the world does, but we are probably wrong about that. Henry Kissinger reminds us China was among the most powerful countries in the world when the U.S. was being settled by Pilgrims. They see that as a normal condition. These people ruled the entire world at one point, or at least the part that was settled and kept records. They weren't a democracy then, and democracy does not suit them.

So, China will probably be doing things the way the rest of the world does then, unless the rest of world is coming around to the Chinese way of looking at things. We are going to have differences for generations. The Russians are stagnant right now and not ones to get caught up in expensive adventures. But what Paul Harvey used to call "the rest of the story" is that China is not waiting around for the rest of the world to come to their way of doing things. They are building the world the way they want it to be. The way they are doing it, this time, is a new kind of war.

I certainly do not mean a missile-throwing, shell-pounding kind of war over territory that someone is going to get when it is over. It is not that kind of war.

It doesn't look like war, and it doesn't fit some of the old definitions, but it hardly matters now that war has changed in ways that we will find uncomfortable and dangerous. Jomini, Von Clausewitz, Giap, Rommel, Sun Tzu, Patton, Genghis Khan, and the many others who are the authorities would be hard-pressed to apply their advice on how to wage war without armies, borders, enemies, or combat in any sense of the word. But, that is what we have, and it certainly is not a war by the historical definition. Maybe, this is partly why we don't have wars anymore. The definition of war doesn't work as well as it used to.

War

It has been 179 years since Von Clausewitz wrote his book, and at least for the last 70 years, we seem to have run out of wars, even ones where the two sides line up with guns and start shooting at each other. Maybe, if we don't call it war, it will somehow be better for everyone.

General Jomini, one of Napoleon's finest, thought the first principle of war was to throw the mass of the army on a military objective, and we still do that now and again. Afghanistan has some of those places, but not many. We had to learn to fight a different kind of war to fight there, but it was clear that we were at war. The Taliban and their allies were on one side and the NATO Allies on the other. As we get closer to leaving the place, the sides become less clear. This is not the war the Chinese would fight. They view war differently.

China's First Principle of War is to never be at war with anyone.

Congress has to declare war, for it to be war in the formal sense of it, but we haven't been having wars like that since World War II. So, we can almost say that we are not at war with anyone either. We must be conflicted about this with Korea, Iraq and Afghanistan certainly looking like wars, the way history defines them, but Congress not being inclined to call it that. Whatever you call it, it is the use of force to compel an enemy to fulfill our will; otherwise, we would not be there.

- The Russians and NATO have both fought what looks like war with the Taliban in Afghanistan.
- Argentina and the United Kingdom fought over some God-forsaken islands and that was a shooting war with missiles and bombs.
- In May of 2011, we have aircraft bombing Libya and ground forces shooting at each other on both sides. This looks like war too, but nobody has called any of these things war.

We seem to be confused about it. It isn't surprising, given our history, that we don't have war anymore. We just have military actions directed by the president. He sends a few hundred people into Uganda with next to no warning to anyone but those who are going. "Surprise," he says. Presidents, regardless of their politics, have been willing to do the kind of things that make war without calling them that. It is still a war, even if you just call it a conflict. It is just that nobody does war anymore.

We also have a difficult time deciding who the enemy might be in these conflicts. We have trouble figuring out if they are at war with us, or with anyone else, for that matter. Terrorist groups, dictators, gangs of thugs and killers, thieves and extortionists can confuse us when we are at war, because we never know if we are at war with them, or not. Sometimes, they are just hanging out where a war might be; sometimes they are just trying to benefit from the confusion; sometimes they are fighting alongside one side or the other. Those of you who saw, or read, *Blackhawk Down* know what I'm talking about. It was easier when the armies lined up and everyone could tell that they were going to make war. "Shoot the ones in the Blue uniforms," my Virginia ancestors used to say.

We are already at war, but all the confusion about what war has become has caused us to miss it. It just isn't the information war that our military leaders had planned, and it doesn't look very much like a traditional war. Mr. Kissinger recently said that if we aren't careful, we will end up in Cold War with China, but he is probably too late with that kind of advice. We are already beyond a Cold War and into an information war with them, and they are playing much better than we are. It is partly because they adapted something we invented, and are doing it better than we are, á la the Japanese picking up continuous improvement processes made famous by Demming, and making them their own. The Chinese are good at Information War.

Information War

In 1995, Winn Schwartau, who had just written a book called *Information Warfare*, was walking ahead of us with our Canadian hosts. My wife had been listening to him speak part of the day and she was anxious to draw some conclusions about what he had been saying. She said, kind of nonchalantly, "He doesn't seem to know very much about information warfare does he?" Winn has sharp ears and stopped almost in mid stride to wait for us to catch up. He ingratiated himself to my wife by starting with "Young lady" and then adding something more unexpected. "You are right about that. I don't know as much about it as some of the people, like your husband, but I can do more in a day to wake people up than he can do in a year. I'm going to go to Europe tomorrow and we are going to hack some Defense Department computers, live, on national television." They guy knew how to make a point.

It wasn't war, but it did compel a few people to want to make changes to the way they did security of their systems in the Pentagon. It wasn't the massing of an army to attack the decisive points of a battlefield that can compel someone to act as you would want. He was using the

Internet to communicate with masses of people about hacking in the information age. Some of those people worked in Defense and some of them on the Hill. This is not classic war, but it is information war. You have to like the guy for practicing what he preaches.

Winn understood an idea that was posed by Marshall McLuhan in 1964. McLuhan said the medium is the message, and almost everyone has heard that at one point and wondered what he was talking about. He said television and its way of spreading ideas and images changed the way people interact. He said to look for more than just the message to see what is happening because of it. Television's ability to make a message through an image is part of that. We saw them coming every day from Viet Nam and did not like what we were seeing. The Internet has a similar capability but it gives more than moving pictures. We are past television as it existed years ago. I watch television on my iPad part of the time, so where you watch the image does not determine what television is anymore; you don't need a television to watch it. The Internet is a medium, like television, and it has changed the way we watch video and changed the way we fight a war.

Some people will go so far as to try to present the Internet as a weapon. When some nickel-and-dime dictator runs out with a camera crew to show a child who was killed when a bomb missed him and hit her, it may have the impact of a weapon, but it isn't one; it is just a medium of showing what has happened. The images of the child are the weapon to change behavior. Now any cell phone anywhere can make one. We may be a little more careful about target verification and take more time to be sure, which will let a few people who should be bombed get away. The people we fight usually don't take as much time to make sure of their targets. That is how this type of Information War changes us a little bit.

The First Information War

The First Information War was not a war at all. It was the created dream of the U.S. military, mostly to get money for its computer systems. Though they may not have known what they had when they put together the ideas, they eventually figured it out. Hundreds of people got involved in things they had no business doing, because it was new and most of the world had never seen Information War. It was a new field to most of them doing it, and it was fairly easy to get to know it. But they really did not have much of an idea about what Information War was (and is), and you won't either, if you expect to get it in this book.

There is a good reason for that. Information War is mostly secret. There is not much anyone can say in the open press about what is real Information War, especially what we have the capability of doing and what the Chinese are actually doing. The only way you can know for sure is to read a whole lot of classified intelligence reports, and then you will just know what the analysts who specialize in this kind of thing believe is true. So, the best I can do here is tell you what I see the Chinese doing and how it relates to Information War. It isn't exactly what military doctrine described, and it certainly is not being applied like most military people think about it. All they know is the kind of war they still teach in school. My school stopped at the Second World War and asked us to read the part about Korea later.

The problem with publishing wide-open journals and policy documents for everyone to see is that anyone above the rank of sergeant starts thinking they know what they are doing and wants to be involved. Now, everybody thinks they can do Information Warfare. All they have to do is follow the steps. It is not that simple, and the rules are changing faster than the policies.

The military's information technology (IT) people thought this was a wonderful thing. We could use computers to actually enhance the war capabilities of the troops. I wanted to play *America the Beautiful* at a couple of these meetings, when they were telling us all the great and wonderful things they could do to help us. The logic was simple. When something is a "force multiplier," the term used most often to describe the benefits of computers for the military commanders, it can be purchased and used as if it were a weapon, even if it isn't. This is done with the belief that the military can then be smaller, but still maintain its strength. Who would say no to something like that?

The catch was, the military did not get smaller, and the IT needs grew until they are the largest share of the $75 billion federal IT budget. There is faulty logic in there somewhere. The only ones who benefited were the offices of all those IT people, mostly because the people buying those computers do not know anything at all about the practice of war. They are just using computers to build an empire.

In *The Changing Role of Information in Warfare* (RAND, 1999), we are told that information will make the military stronger by leveraging and synthesizing the capabilities that already exist. "Toward the more expansive end are those who see the 'information sphere' becoming the battlefield of the future — where the main battle will not be fought over territory using physical force, but over the minds of the combatants and their access to information." Glorious.

It sounds like some pie-in-the-sky thinking those generals were reading in Antietam before they sent their soldiers across a narrow bridge into a line of Confederate sharpshooters. They won in the end, but everyone today wonders how. The worst part of this whole thing is that RAND and the Department of Defense were right about what they put together. It is turning out to be war that we should already know all about. In the last 10 years we have just forgotten about it.

Early on in this, the military started calling what they did information operations, to imply that they were massing information in the way we used to mass troops, so it could be applied wherever it was needed. It is a mushy concept that is easy to say and really hard to do. Most military people do not understand the concept and don't apply it when they do. They build a lot of networks, but they don't manage their information very well. They say they believe, but they don't act like it. They have made loads of paper and Powerpoint slides that sounded like they were going to revolutionize warfare. They continue to buy more and more computers, with the idea that they will make them an agile but smaller force. They got quite a bit bigger, but they weren't fighting an Information War.

The military doctrine, the part of this that is supposed to be read and applied, was summarized, in 1995, as a complex mix of things that are hardly related, but all use information, or information systems, in some way to deny an enemy some capability. This is what some people call "total war," the mixing of combat operations with disruption and control of economic and political functions of government. This is, by the way, what requires centralized control that the military used to have. They seem to have lost it somewhere along the way. We generally don't see war this way, but some of our military planners do.

What we have been missing for the past 10 years is the Chinese are implementing this strategy of war, using a basic policy of never being at war with anyone. They want to win without firing a shot, and they are going about it the right way.

2

Economic War

Economics is not normally thought of as a part of war, but it has always been. In the big picture, if an intelligence service collects information about the strategy a trade delegation will use, and it provides that information to its own country's trade delegation, that is economic warfare. So, if one of the countries interested in hosting the World Cup decides it would like to know how all the other bidders were going to structure their bids, they can put the intelligence service on to trying to find out. A government can also collect intelligence and give it to its private industry. They could just as easily use government officials to try to influence the award of a contract for airplanes, a new national wireless system, or retrofitting of ships. Or, a country can just lower or raise the value of its currency a little. The Chinese are better at this than anyone, although a few other countries might want to debate that. Russia got the 2018 World Cup and the FBI is investigating how those bids might have been compromised.

There are grey lines here. One country might think using government officials to influence contracts is OK if they don't pay bribes to anyone. Another country night think bribes are part of business, so it would be foolish not to pay them. Where there are loads of grey is something like the award of the Air Force tanker program to an EU company called Airbus. There was such hoopla about it that the Air Force had to re-compete the contract so Boeing could win. As far as we know, no bribes were paid to anyone here, but the award of a big contract to an overseas company tells us a little about how important these big contracts are to the national security of a country. When there is cheating going on and the trade imbalances reflect it, it can be seen as war of a different sort.

This type of war with China started longer ago than you might think. At the time we were putting together the strategy for an Information War, China was not ready to fight and the Russians were. The Russians will fight most anytime a war comes up and they don't have a great track record because of it. The Chinese fight when the time is right for them. They waited.

I am old enough to remember the Russian Premier Khrushchev banging a shoe on his desk at the UN, saying, "We will bury you." It was scary. It was the kind of in-your-face blustering we had seen before from Russia, but we believed they had enough nuclear weapons to bury us all. He said, to paraphrase Stalin, we would sell him the rope that he would use to hang us. We all knew what he was talking about. Business traders do not care as much about politics as they do about profit. A few of them will trade with the devil to keep a company afloat in hard times. They may pretend they didn't know it was the devil, but they won't ask very many questions about the clues they see.

We fought a Cold War with Russia and I must admit, it was great. The military kept busy and the Department of Defense did very well during that time. Most of my career we battled them in one way or another and both sides were better for it. A defector told me once I was naïve about how the Cold War actually worked, and after he explained it, I understood that I may have been. He had been in Russia while I was over here in the U.S. We were fighting each other before he defected and started helping us.

He was in countermeasures, a dark business of watching what the enemy is doing and trying to come up with ways of defeating them by undermining their capabilities. If I fly into Russian airspace, and I know what frequency their radars work on, I can build a jammer that will let me stop them from using those radars to detect me, until I can attack them. The Russians are pretty smart about these things so they want to build radars that won't easily be jammed so they make them hop around on the radar spectrum so my jammer can't pin them down. When I see them making such a thing, I want to jam more frequencies those radars operate in. This is a simple explanation of something a lot more complicated. Every frequency we jam, we can't use anymore, so the number of available frequencies gets pretty small after 25 years of this.

He asked me a question. "Do you remember that you used to tell your companies not to test their equipment outside when the Russian satellites were overhead?" I did remember that. "Well, our Russian defense forces used to tell us the same thing, when your satellites came

over. Did we stop testing outside because we were told not to?" I assumed
they did. "Of course we did not!" he said, slapping me on the back with
a good-natured whack. "We still tested our things when your satellites
were watching. Then your people would see what we were doing and
they would start working on countermeasures for our weapons. Then
your people would test outside when our satellites were over your head
and we got to see what you were doing. If either one of us had stopped,
the Cold War would have been over for both of us." Cynical, I was thinking.

The Chinese have taken the same principles and applied them to
business, to make that business part of their war. They have a law that
says businesses do not get a license and start operating in China just
because they want to. China has rules. They want to trade, and we know
they do quite a bit of that, but they don't want to trade a few computers
for an earthmoving truck from Caterpillar. What they want to trade for
is the ability to make those earthmoving trucks. They want us to teach
them to make the rope that they will use to hang us, which is one better
than the Russians in Khrushchev's time. We have a large number of businesses that are willing to help them do it.

In the Cold War we understood what Russia was trying to do, so
we cut back on some of our trade, particularly in areas where there might
be some military benefit to them. We don't seem to see China the same
way.

In order to get in the Chinese market, the business has to give them
something of value, a technology that will be shared with their Chinese
counterpart. China says we only do this in about 20 percent of the cases,
but there is no way to say, one way or another. The percentages are not
as important as the use to which these are put.

When GM was negotiating to bring the Chevy Volt, their hybrid,
into the country, they wanted to sell the Volt and get subsidies given to
those companies that share technology. What the Chinese offered them
was a government subsidy of $19,000 per car. That is a lot of money.
But, GM has been in China for a long time and they know their way
around.

GM had built a car called the Spark and China's biggest automobile
maker, Chery, started building a similar car called the QQ. They look
quite a bit alike. Admittedly, the names are not even close, but GM
claimed the exterior and interior of the QQ looked a lot like the Spark.

GM filed a complaint with the Chinese government that Chery had copied exactly the design of the GM Spark. The commerce minister said they did not provide "certain," meaning exact, evidence that it had been copied, which is not always like evidence you will see the CSI folks come up with on television. When Audi sued a company in China for making a car that looked a lot like the Audi 5000, the Chinese court said the flag on the front of the car proved it was different. The two cars may look alike, but they have a few small differences.[1] Given that experience, GM said no to the subsidies for the Volt. That effectively increases the cost of the car by that $19,000, and makes it more difficult for it to compete in the market.

The high-speed trains, one of which crashed this year, were adapted by Chinese companies after Kawasaki Heavy Industries, Ltd., Siemens AG, Alstom SA and Bombardier, Inc. helped them develop the technologies. China says it has adapted and improved these designs and used them to compete. That is certainly a good reason for keeping the press from covering the train wreck. Their trains are faster and more efficient. The people they are competing with say the designs were used in violation of agreements established by their companies. China says it is great to be able to compete in this market. There are hundreds of similar stories about China's trade. They use it to steal technology and compete against the people they got it from. They think the world owes them the right to use whatever they get. It may not be fair, but it works for them.

Apple, the company that makes my Mac, iPad and iPhone, uses a third of a company called Hon Hai Precision Industry, also known as, Foxconn. Foxconn has 800,000 employees, more than the combined employment for Apple, Dell, Microsoft, HP, Intel and Sony. They made the national news this year when Apple called in the press to take a field trip to the site making iPads. They also make my Xbox, my Intel motherboard and quite a few other things too. They are not competing with anyone on what they build. They are good at it; they have produced a hot product, with high quality, probably faster than most other companies of the world could do, but it comes at a price.

Foxconn is probably best known for Apple and the number of suicides its employees have managed to accomplish in the past year. The factory that makes my iPad is not a happy place. Eighteen people jumped to their deaths from high buildings in the Foxconn complex and 20 others were stopped from jumping by nets put up around the building. They have labor problems every day, but no lack of labor, much of it from outside China.

Not the kind of place that makes a person think of the brushed walls of the Apple campus in Cupertino, where iPads are not made, but Apple keeps them as their manufacturing arm anyway. The simple matter is, they keep up with the schedule and demands of production, even though it may cause their people stress beyond what we might want or tolerate. We could use the same logic on child labor or prostitution, but we don't. Let some country try to make tennis shoes using children in sweat shops where they have to work 12 hour days and there will be an uproar like they were killing those kids. But we have a business were the stress is killing people and it is an internal problem for them. There must be a difference there somewhere.

The stress of it has finally produced inspections by the Fair Labor Association, an industry group that helps to set standards for the industries they are inspecting. We saw everyone in a uniform on the Foxconn floor, and those uniforms all looked new. Maybe, in such a controlled society, it is the only way to get the wages increased and the working conditions improved, which it did. Apple is paying for that.

In 2010, Intel added its first manufacturing facility in China. They manufacture chipsets and memory, two of the fundamental components of computers. The chip manufacturing facility is the size of 23 football fields but uses slightly older technology than Intel uses in the U.S. because of export restrictions. They have several research and development facilities included in its $4.7 billion investment, so the Chinese are learning to make, and improve, chips the Intel way. Intel is teaching the Chinese to make chips that are used in computers and almost everything that has small computers in it. Some of the profits of those Intel chips make their way back to the USA, so the board of Intel can say what is good for China is also good for the U.S. Depending on how you feel about a 10 to 1 ratio of jobs in their favor, you might even agree with the thinking there.

If you also need software, the Chinese are learning how to make software from Microsoft. When the Chinese president visited the U.S. in January 2011, the current CEO of Microsoft was there too. President Obama pointed out that 90 percent of Microsoft software used in China was pirated. This is probably not the way to start a state visit, but it does articulate the problem pretty clearly.

When Microsoft first started in China it was having a terrible time with pirated software and tried to deal with it as it had everywhere else in the world, by suing. They lost in court regularly, because Chinese law does not protect intellectual property the way laws in most other countries do. But suing gave them a bad reputation. Someone who sues to get their way, even though they weren't getting that either, is frowned upon equally in the universe. They got frustrated and went through five changes of Chinese leadership in their operations in five years.

The Chinese were starting to try out some new software, Linux, that was public domain. Linux is pretty good software and it has all kinds of applications that do well at most office functions. If the Chinese decided to adopt that kind of software, they might not have all the features of a Microsoft, but they would have the right price. They can make decisions like that because they are a government-managed, central-planning, one party system. We can't even do this if we have a Democratic president and the House and Senate are both run by the same party.

So Microsoft decided having their software copied was better than not having their software sold there. This is a strange bit of logic. But, what they also did was start cooperating with the Chinese government to help them build a software industry. Eventually, that cooperation resulted in government requiring the use of licensed software for itself, but the pirated software still is a problem for them. The other problem, of course, is that software industry they helped to create may produce software that competes with Microsoft. The decision to do that will come back to haunt them one day. We are seeing a similar turn of events with wind generators and solar panels.

You will remember Solyndra, long after the White House has finished defending themselves against claims of acting in haste to give them a $535 million loan that will now have to be paid back by the taxpayers. The Obama administration filed a complaint against China with the World Trade Organization because China's Special Fund for Wind Power Manufacturing required recipients of aid to use Chinese-made parts and amounted to a subsidy. After the complaint was brought, the Chinese stopped funding the subsidy. In the meantime, though, they were giving $30 billion in loans to their wind and solar companies, 20 times what the U.S. gives. This is the benefit of a centralized, managed economy. It is easier to move money around and control a market. If that fails, they are not above cheating.

American Superconductor Corporation (AMSC), which makes management software for wind turbines, filed suit in China in 2011, saying a government-controlled Chinese company, Sinovel, stole its designs for power management and competed with them for wind generation equipment. In their latest update in 2013, China's highest court is looking at jurisdiction now, since the case was thrown out by a lower court. Sinovel made the turbines; AMSC made the power management systems that helped them work together. The person pleading guilty to giving the information to Sinovel was a Serb engineer working in Austria for the subsidiary of a U.S. company. This was a real international case. He stopped working for AMSC in March, but maintained computer accounts which gave him access. In April, Sinovel stopped accepting shipments from AMSC, claiming it was reducing inventory, and stopped paying for any more products from them. AMSC is clearly not happy about it. They say that a senior level employees of Sinovel actually paid for the goods that were stolen from them. Now, Sinovel has it all and doesn't need to buy it from anyone. With few "improvements" like the high-speed trains made, they can be off and running. It doesn't bother them that the technology was stolen.

An update to this story[2] says this matter was brought to the future leader of China's government in his visit in February 2012. It listed the value of the goods lost by AMSC at $700 million, and their shares dropped 80 percent. Sinovel paid $1.5 million to the thief who took the technology. Sinovel countersued in China for $58 million for "breach of contract." This continues to hold the interest of the administration, which was said to have published a background paper on this case for the visit because it was "so egregious."

Pfizer is moving its anti-bacterial research to China. This is not the manufacturing business, but the research end of the operations and is a first in that. They are talking about doing clinical trials of drugs in China, but this is only the beginning of pharmaceuticals. The critical ingredients for most antibiotics are now made in China. Most of the large penicillin fementers are in China because the government, in the early '80s made an effort to grow their share of the market. Almost half of the generic drug applications made to the FDA are from China.

So far, I do not seem to have a problem with that, but I'm not taking heparin which keeps my blood from clotting when it is not supposed to. A couple of years ago there were two large manufacturers of heparin, Baxter International and APP Pharmaceuticals. Federal regulators figured out that Baxter's supplies had been contaminated by a Chinese supplier. They didn't figure this out because they went to China to inspect them; they figured it out when four people died and some others got sick. They decided it might be a good idea to start getting heparin from APP but they found it hard to ignore that APP's supplier was also in China. Having all those generic drugs in my day-to-day pill box now makes me nervous. There are so many manufacturing arms moving to China, we can't keep up with how those relate. If they are manufacturing chips used in aircraft autopilots, they might be manufacturing chips used in military aircraft autopilots. We might find that is not such a good idea if it turns out we have to go to war with them one day.

They will have the same feeling about the growth and potential of COMAC, the Commercial Aircraft Corporation of China. While the Chinese learn to build airplanes the way Boeing and Airbus do, they are not competing with them — yet — because they make single-aisle planes where Canada's Bombardier and Brazil's Embraer are the main manufacturers. These two companies must feel good about having Boeing and Airbus help China build up their competition while selling them the big jets. GE supplies the avionics for these aircraft, so they will learn to build them from one of the best. But, the government intent is to compete with them one day, and judging from the past, that day will not be far off. We will eventually have an aircraft industry, automobile industries, drug manufacturing, software, and a host of others that will compete, because that is the only way China will have it.

To be fair, companies go into this with their eyes open. They know the rules, including those that say that a Chinese company must be selected as a partner to operate in China, and they know what they have to do to get into the markets there. They also, unless they get really bad advice, know their technology will be stolen. It goes with the territory. The Chinese have a different understanding of intellectual property. They think they should be allowed to use it, if they have it, no matter how they came by it. They don't feel too bad about opening up a complete counterfeit store, Apple logo and all.

You may think the Chinese are just good players of the game, so they win. That would be wrong. The Chinese make new rules to make the game harder for people who are playing against them and they don't play by anybody else's rules. They cheat.

The U.S. has never had a policy to share its intelligence with the commercial businesses of the country, when so many other countries do it. With the businesses in China being state-owned, the distinctions are harder to manage. When a trade delegation complains that the Chinese were negotiating from our end position, they know those end positions were compromised. The reasons are varied but a businessman traveling in China noticed his handheld computer had been compromised with software that would "phone home" if connected to another network when he got back to his office. Dr. Joel Brenner, national counter–Intelligence executive, said when a business traveler goes to China, he should have a throw-away cell phone, which cuts down on the opportunities to get into other people's networks — if you actually throw it away.

One network security specialist said some of his Fortune 500 clients traveling to China had software planted on their computers and their networks in the U.S. routinely mapped by the Chinese. This is not new and Russians did the same thing before them. They probably don't see this as anything they should not be allowed to do. They believe everyone does it.

In a few countries of the world, as any world traveler knows, you cannot leave your hotel room without someone taking a look at what you have on your computer. This has becomes so blatant, that most places hardly even try to hide the fact that they have been there. Planting software that phones home is a relatively new off-shoot of that, but not surprising. It was a natural evolution of spying.

However, as trade becomes both an offensive and defensive weapon to exert influence, what is done in the name of keeping trade going has exceeded what we usually expect in the business world. There are other countries who do the same types of things, but for sheer in-your-face stealing, you can't beat China. This year was the first time in a long time that a senior Administration official, like the treasury secretary, acknowledged in public the Chinese were stealing us blind. Some people see this as a very competitive nature of Chinese business people, but there are other names that can be applied to it. They want to win, because that is part of the strategy of economic war.

Global Domination

To win the war, the Chinese have to be dominate in ways we understand. That doesn't mean that they only trade with the U.S., because it isn't just the U.S. that they want to be dominant over. They are making a profit of about $300 billion every year, and in the zero sum game of trade, they take that from the rest of the world. Sometimes, the rest of the world is not happy about it; sometimes, they are glad to have the trade.

We have to suspend our understanding of the Communist system to believe that Chinese business is just like any other business in the world. They are not like us. We confuse Chinese businesses with our businesses and they are careful to keep up that illusion. They incorporate subsidiaries in other countries. They establish boards with members of the Communist Party in senior positions. They write bylaws and hold board meetings that can be seen by everyone. They have their companies act like they are independent of government control.

But, even their public companies are not "open" in any sense of the word. Try and find out anything substantive about the managers of any Chinese company, and you will know what I'm talking about. There is very little to see, except smoke. The Security and Exchange Commission recently opened inquiries in on its third Chinese company for what is a very complicated scheme that avoids oversight of their companies that comes from operating a public company in the U.S. Everyone saw how this oversight can cause companies like Facebook to get trampled in the market. The SEC is looking at the practice of "reverse mergers" where a Chinese firm merges with a shell company in the U.S. so it doesn't get the scrutiny given to companies forming an initial public offering — particularly, the accounting. Third parties start trading in the shell company, raising its ability to get financing. The *Wall Street Journal* article says several of these "companies have had trading in their shares suspended or seen their outside auditors resign over the past year."[3] This isn't good business; it is potentially a criminal case that proves the Chinese are more than willing to do business outside the norm expected of a publicly traded company. They have done worse things.

The *Financial Times* reported in September that in 2004, the largest mobile phone company in the world, China Mobile, was having a difficult time helping investors understand their leadership change. The Mr. Wang, who everyone thought was the number one guy, was replaced as the head of the Communist Party at the state-owned parent company. The parallel to this in our system would be that the CEO of AT&T held two offices, one the head of the Democratic Committee in that area of business, and the other as CEO. The job as head of the Democratic Committee was higher up in the food chain than his CEO job. And, there was only one party — no Republicans. The decision was made by something called the Central Organization Department, which does not justify its decisions to anyone. Mr. Wang is replaced at the senior position and transferred to another supposedly independent company run by the same bunch. Now, he is not as well placed. If I had been an investor in China Mobile, I would have concerns.

It pays to know what the other businesses in China are up to, and have the political connections to smooth over conflicts with government officials. Ask Rio Tinto and Walmart.[4]

Rio Tinto is one of the largest mining companies in the world and is based in the U.K. It does business in aluminum, copper, diamonds, iron ore, and energy and has 77,000 employees, some in China. In March of 2010, four of its employees were sentenced to between 7 and 14 years for accepting bribes and stealing commercial secrets. That last part is the reason for concern, since it is a fine line between a state-owned secret and a commercial secret, when the businesses they were selling to were state-owned.

Rio Tinto admits they took bribes, which is more common in some parts of the world than others. In China, gift giving seems to be an institution among government officials and business leaders, and it is sometimes hard to make the distinction between something meant to influence and something that is like a business lunch or Christmas gift in this country. They took money and were expected to act in a certain way as a result. There is not much grey in that.

But, in most of the globe, there is a difference between business secrets and state secrets. If a person knowingly pays for either one, that usually isn't bribery. That can be theft of intellectual property or espionage. State secrets are usually marked in some way that identifies them as "Restricted," "Top Secret" or some other type of thing that can tip off a person that they might be protected by the government. China doesn't always do that, and to make it worse, tends to use the term "state secret" to mean "whatever we say." This makes it harder for anyone to tell, and has caused foreign companies to start getting rid of some of their documents, just in case they fit into the new category.

That isn't what the case was really about. The Chinese seem intent on making it more difficult for foreign companies to do business in their country. They want them to be successful first, then make it difficult to compete. Under new rules, foreign companies may be prosecuted for obtaining financial, investment, managerial, and organizational information about state-owned *competitors*. Getting that type of information is usually business intelligence and is not a crime. In 2010, an American geologist was sentenced to eight years in prison for purchasing publicly available geologic reports that Chinese authorities retroactively deemed to be state secrets. It is the "retroactively" part of it that is tricky.

Doing business becomes much more interesting if you can't collect information from government-owned businesses or the government itself, without violating some law somewhere, and that is exactly what they were charged with. The court said they caused China to pay more for iron ore than they should have had to pay. That part may even be true, but in some places that is called "smart business," not a crime. It is probably the same when they overcharge us for something they made, but you don't see any of their people going to jail for it.

In the end, they decided to charge them with stealing commercial secrets, not state secrets. People who steal state secrets don't last very long, and can have spectacular trials, when they are public. The trial still took several months, but it was low-key. They made their point.

They are doing the same thing with Walmart by arresting people and fining them $400,000 for selling pork as organic when it wasn't. I hardly know what "organic" is anymore and they are arresting people for selling something because it wasn't. After one gang member got a suspended death sentence for forcing people to buy water-injected pork, you might have thought pork was more important there than in some places.

While the approach is supposed to be related to a food safety issue in China, after some really nasty chemically treated pork was being sold in other stores, it could be any number of things that were really behind it. Walmart got fined $500,000 for charging too much for certain types of goods and not doing their part to keep down inflation. It is more likely the continued pressure on foreign firms which makes it more difficult for them to operate there. The Chinese are glad to take investment money from them, expand their operations until they learn to compete with them, then tighten down their profits and take over the business. This should sound familiar to anyone who watches television. This is the Mafia business model, the "Tony" Soprano *modus operandi* with the Communist government being the senior leadership.

The Mafia was into all kinds of activity that could seriously get them in trouble. They loaned money at low rates to people they like, or higher rates to those who weren't family. They helped the business expand and allowed other people who were also family to buy into their operations. They branched out into legitimate businesses to handle money and cover their operations. They sent their kids to the best schools to have them learn how to do this well. They were subsidizing the best schools with so many of them going there. They kept everything in the family. It is cozy, and very, very communistic. (The Mafia probably wouldn't like that analogy, so I add that it was not my intent to infer that the Mafia is, in any way, Communist.) This can be summarized in the interesting case of the 88 Queensway Group, a big, supposedly "private" firm.

When the U.S.–China Economic and Security Review Commission did a check of investments in Angola (they were trying to figure out if these were profit making business deals of strategic government investments), they found a few companies operating from the same address in Hong Kong, but they had never been linked in the press or business circles. A few individuals were controlling some small companies from the same street address, 10/F Two Pacific Place, 88 Queensway, Hong Kong.

One person who was not well known in financial circles was a director in 34 of the companies. Her husband was tied to two state-owned companies, one of which was very closely linked to Chinese intelligence and served as a cover for agents operating outside the country. Another officer's residence was listed at the same location as the Ministry of State Security, which is home to China's foreign intelligence collection. Of course, this was a coincidence.

Several of its key personnel have ties to China International Trust and Investment Company (CITIC), China National Petrochemical Corporation (Sinopec), and possibly China's Intelligence Services. We have to remember that a close look at most of the businesses of the world will show some relationships like this from former government officials. They had jobs before they moved on the board of directors or became vice president of marketing for that airplane. This is what qualifies them for the position. In this case, though, there were some differences from a "normal business."

The group also had gotten high-level access to the governments and national oil companies of the countries where it puts its money. In order to get oil or construction projects in Angola, a company has to go through the Export-Import Bank of China and, by terms of those contracts, has to be mostly Chinese. The oil construction contracts gave guarantees of oil deliveries as collateral. This is a cozy arrangement for China and makes them the envy of many oil companies.

Two Chinese financing companies provide most of the money for those projects through arrangements with the Angola government's Ministry of Finance. Those companies have separate agreements for some other functions of other government agencies operating businesses in Angola. This kind of contact wording would attract attention almost anywhere in the business world, and probably says as much about the Angola government as it does Chinese business.

Soon after it started some of these companies, the group began entering into joint ventures using some of its interesting connections in the Congo, Venezuela, Angola, and the Russian diamond business. The 88 Queensway Group has established over thirty different holding companies and subsidiaries to do its investing. In addition to Angola, it has operations in sub–Saharan Africa, Latin America, Southeast Asia and the United States. In the U.S. it was briefly on the radar screen in 2008 for purchases of the J.P. Morgan Chase Building in Manhattan, 49 percent of the former New York Times Building, and 49 percent of the Clock Tower, also in Manhattan.[5]

Nothing tells more about the synergy between government officials, their spouses, and business dealings that enrich them than the growing case of a British businessman, Neil Heywood, found dead in a less-than impressive hotel near his best customer and mentor, Gu Kailai, wife of a high ranking Party official, Bo Xalai.[6] Nothing has stirred the politics and business relations of two countries more than the flap that came out of this mess. It was historic.

Bo Xalai is not just another party official; he was talked about as one of the leaders who would take a seat on the nine-member council that runs the country in the somewhat the same way the U.S. cabinet runs ours. We have more people and less power, but it is close enough for governments. Remember that this is a Communist country and the centralized control is much more rigid than in the bureaucracies of the world.

Bo Xalai may not get that seat now because it appears, without accusing anyone, that his wife may have had Mr. Heywood poisoned, then covered it up by having his body disposed of before an autopsy could be conducted. This is generally frowned on almost anywhere, but seemed to be close to being accepted until the whole thing was upset by the local chief of police going to the U.S. Consulate in Chengdu. You can imagine the chief of police in Chicago driving over to Rockville to the Chinese consulate and turning himself in to report a crime. The Chinese would be dumbfounded and might take a few days to figure out what to do. That is about what happened here. After the smoke settled, anonymous reports started to come in, and a few have been very accurate. Someone close to the action is talking.

The police chief was a political embarrassment to the U.S because he was in a position to know what actually happened; his police actually investigated the case. He was eventually persuaded to seek shelter with Chinese and leave the U.S. out of it. This is international politics at its finest and has nothing to do with war, but it shows the lengths diplomats will go to. Diplomats want peace at the expense of any local official, though surely we will hear the whole wonderful story one day. For diplomacy to succeed, it must be wrapped in a package of friendship, with smiles all around.

He must have felt that he was expendable, abandoned by Bo and Gu Xalai and looking at a case causing an international uproar, since the British wanted to know what happened to Mr. Heywood. They were reading the newspaper reports and diplomatic cables flying everywhere and they wanted to get more from the official sources. You might sympathize with the Consulate, having someone like this showing up on the doorstop, but that is why they are trained to represent us.

The police chief proved impossible to cover up. People started to poke around and reporters began calling their sources. The more that came out, the worse it got. This started to filter up to the highest reaches of government when Bo Xalai was removed as Choungqing Communist Party secretary, the main base of his power. This is a little like the president removing the director of the General Services Administration, except that she would have been in the running for vice president in the next election. Bo's wife's power comes from businesses she operates. She was then under arrest, which seriously influenced how far her businesses would go, and how much "management" she could do from jail, where those skills would be tested.

The best information about this case does not come from the Chinese government, as we might expect, but from a website called boxun.com, that is outside the Golden Shield.[7] (In spite of it being in Chinese, this site is good read. Google does a decent job of translation and the issues can be roughly followed.) It is in the United States and operated by a fellow named Watson Meng, from the hotbed of political reporting in Durham, North Carolina. That makes it harder to control and much less responsive to censorship. However, as with most people critical of China, the site is now under attack, presumably by people who are, or were, allies of Bo. Bo's enemies feed the site and his friends attack it. Not something most people want to be caught up in, much to Meng's credit. That is real journalism.

Meng's site is dangerous territory for the informants, who must be known to factions in the government. The Chinese government is making every effort to distinguish this as a "criminal act" and not part of any dealings the government itself was involved in. Bo was said to have been involved in this act, and so removed, to be prosecuted. We see the same type of political response to the prosecution of the former presidential candidate John Edwards, who was accused of misusing campaign funds to support a mistress and his child. One of his aides even tried to claim paternity for the child to keep it from the newspapers. Bo is criminalized and the taint does not extend back to the Central Committee, which was willing to accept him until he became involved in a crime that nobody is accusing him of committing.

The political intrigue is about all we see, but the business fallout will not take much longer. Her companies will have less chance for contracts and trade that depended on her husband's name. In the business community, people stop inviting these folks to power lunches and that little get together at the club. They forget names of relatives, friends, children and pets. There was some discussion about removing Bo's son from Harvard, even though he was supposed to graduate in the same month. His sports car might be downgraded to something a little less expensive. Those special privileges are the first thing to go, and it looks like the bandwagon is rolling.

Look at the way Queenway is constructed and match it up with how this case is unfolding. It describes the way politics and business are related and how quickly one or the other can be undone, when the timing is right. The Chinese might say, "This happens everywhere in the world,"

World Trade Imbalance with China

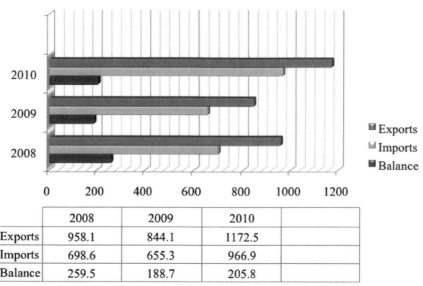

	2008	2009	2010	
Exports	958.1	844.1	1172.5	
Imports	698.6	655.3	966.9	
Balance	259.5	188.7	205.8	

Billions of Euros

The Chinese have a trade surplus with the world, though the amounts fluctuate from year to year. These figures are in billions of Euros, with the Euro being about $1.25 (International Monetary Fund [Director of Trade Statistics — DoTS]).

and they would be right, but it seldom leads to murder. It also is a clear light on the spouses of Party officials who seem to mix business with politics every day. It is difficult to separate the two.

From such humble beginnings come greatness, backed by financing from the national government. By staying private, companies like those belonging to Gu avoid the disclosures required of most public companies trying to operate in those parts of the world, and ours. The Chinese understand the relationships between government and business and they are open about how it works inside the country. They keep it all in the family.

The 27 countries of the European Union (EU) got the same warning we did, on the U.S. Congress' attempt to start taxing some of the goods we get from China. When they need influence, they can get it, because they don't just hold Treasury notes in the U.S.; they have about a quarter of their money in EU debt, and they have promised to buy more. They have gotten bonds from Greece, Ireland, Italy, Portugal and Spain at a time when analysts would say these are a bad bet. So, they are either the world's worst investors, or they have something else in mind.

Europe has the same kind of objections to state-supported operations competing with their private business, only they use the World Trade Organization's anti-dumping laws that trigger when they get trade that hurts one of their local industries. Just as an example, there is a series of them for bathroom and paving tiles, as hard as that might be to believe. The EU imposes tariffs as high as 73 percent on these tiles, because they are sold at a cost the EU thinks is illegally subsidized and interferes with an EU industry. They have 49 anti-dumping measures they impose on Chinese goods and the Chinese do not like it very much. We have some, but not many.

There is talk of a trade war, but the difference is, the EU has already started down this road. They put tariffs on glossy paper used in magazines. China is putting tariffs on EU potato starch (no, it doesn't have to make sense) and there are more coming. Traders were already complaining about the Chinese bureaucracy requiring product certifications, different labeling standards, import approval requirements and customs delays. Sometimes, they have higher requirements for foreign imports than they have on their own.

Product certifications are the most interesting from the standpoint of protection of intellectual property. The Chinese require an inspection of the plant where the goods are produced and a certification of the goods by the Chinese government. In some cases, knock-offs of products will show up on the streets of Beijing before they ever formally are accepted, and way before they get into production. That has to be some product certification process they have there. It is clever though. They manage to have a product on the street before a potential competitor can get started.

Investments in telecommunications are required by China's admission into the World Trade Organization, but of the 1600 approved, only 5 had foreign financing. The interest of investors is the growth of their industry, adding 1.25 million cellular subscribers every week. If that seems like a big number, that's because it is. Only equipment manufacturers are allowed to invest there. The EU has complained but the Chinese are saying it is partly a national security issue, and that is plausible without being entirely accurate. It is a national security issue, if it is reciprocal and is a national security issue to everyone. There used to be a saying of the Russians, "What's mine is mine; what's yours is negotiable." There must be a similar Chinese saying since that is how they operate.

China is Africa's biggest trading partner. Sudan, which is not exactly a garden spot of investment opportunities in the last few years, sells most of its oil to China on the same types of arrangements they established in Angola. The Chinese seem to be able to put the war between the North and South of Sudan behind them and live with the government, such that it is. They make headway because they are willing to ignore what governments do with the money they give them, and focus more on trade they get in return. Most of that is oil.

A BBC report says Ethiopia had qualms about China but had to admit they were able to keep costs under control better than most of the other contractors. That means they can perform, not just talk. They got more work as a result. If the Chinese can sell bridges in the U.S., they certainly can do business in Ethiopia doing the same thing. If we don't like it, they won't care.

The copper mines of Zambia have benefited from a $2 billion investment from China but the new president has been critical of its mismanagement of labor. Chinese companies have ignored local labor laws, discouraged unions and strikes and kept pay low for workers. If they weren't Chinese, they would be called colonials.

China is growing business with Brazil and Latin America for raw materials, but the business has not always been good. Brazil has started anti-dumping tariffs on Chinese made synthetic fibers, which they say are being sold at less than production costs, and have clamped down on illegal imports.

Illegal imports are interesting because that can be a pseudonym for "fake." They account for part of the world's trade in counterfeits, and Brazil is not the only place with this problem. It is a slightly different thing from stealing someone's technology and making the goods to compete with them. This is stealing the name of the company and making the product look like an original. We had a fellow in one of our offices who brought back some disks, made in China, that had almost every kind of Microsoft software you could think of on it. It was the right color; it had an instruction manual with it; it had the hologram on it that made it look like the real thing. There were two glaring differences. There was only one box and there were several types of software in it, and it had every virus known to man on one or another, of the disks. One of my marketing professors brought in a Parker pen that looked exactly like the real thing but didn't feel as heavy. The big players in counterfeit merchandise are the high rollers of 5th Avenue and Rodeo Drive, but they can be in high school and come home to video games that are played online. The U.S. claims it loses a billion dollars a year to counterfeit goods made in China, but they are not the only ones who get clipped.

The Chinese make Kawasaki and Honda motorcycles and "clones" of these, BMW, and police motorcycles. A clone is surely not something made under a license, though sometimes it is hard to tell what is made under a license and what is not. Their motorcycles look a lot like the ones made in Japan and Germany, only they aren't.

Everyone knows how the French are about wine. They are very discriminating and refined. When we buy French wine, we assume it is pretty good. Now the Chinese have come up with an interesting way of making the very best French wine, with, of all things, French wine, and it is good wine. They get original bottles from restaurants and copy the labels. Then they buy a good wine and put it in the bottle with the better wine label. Most of us are not French or could not tell the difference.[8]

Sixty Minutes has done a couple of segments on Chinese counterfeiting and they show the scale of what is going on, just from a retail standpoint. The Chinese counterfeited a Harry Potter book that was never written by J.K. Rowling; they just made it up and used her name. They have a 5-story complex that sells almost nothing that is not counterfeit, from golf clubs to blue jeans. It is not illegal to sell "small quantities" of counterfeit goods, so they do that over and over.[9] There is some enforcement for the press and documentation of seizures, but the rest is corrupt. They say it is a cost of doing business in China. The manufacturers of the original goods don't think so, and neither do most of us.

Where this gets dangerous is the manufacture of airplane parts and military supplies. When Callaway Golf Company started getting those fake golf clubs in, they discovered that they looked real, but they were steel instead of titanium, a small but important difference. The shafts were breaking and people were returning them to the place they thought made them. Airplane parts had the same problem a few years ago because some of them were breaking at bad times. It isn't quite so amusing when part of the tail section jams while the plane is taking off.

Singapore, Viet Nam and South Korea have concerns about China too, and there are two things that make that worth considering. It is rare for China to get pushy with its neighbors, but it has with Japan over the East China Sea Islands, which are a long way from the mainland. Second, China is moving work to Viet Nam for its cheaper labor, and they are not exactly enemies. This kind of thing rarely happens in the Friends of China Club.

This is a murky area between China, Taiwan, Japan, Korea and a set of islands just west of Okinawa called the Senkakus Islands. The Chinese have laid out a national boundary line that goes out far enough to take in parts of Japan and all of Taiwan. The Japanese don't think that was the right place to set a line and they keep patrol boats there to make sure nobody starts living there; they think the islands belong to them. China says it found those islands a long time ago and they own them. For a first, Taiwan agrees with them.

We have the same type of problem with California. The Native Americans, Spanish, Mexicans and U.S. all claimed it at one time, but nobody is going back to Spain's rule to make a claim on it. It would be interesting to see what happened if they did.

In a world of strange bedfellows, Viet Nam and India are exploring for oil near those Senkaku islands.

One day in September of 2010, a Chinese fishing boat collided with, or rammed (depending on who is telling the story), one of the patrol boats. Fishing boats are usually found there since it is a huge fishing area, but they usually don't ram another boat. The Japanese took the crew, the captain and the ship and held onto them. Needless to say, the Chinese were not very happy and said they wanted the whole of them back. The Japanese sent the crew back and kept the captain, perhaps with the idea that they might try him under their law.

The Chinese demanded his release. This is diplomatic talk, unless you start getting planes in the air and moving ships into the area. The Japanese said they would talk about it in negotiations. The Chinese said no to that, not wanting to talk. After suitable smoke and fury, they won. They got the captain back, but there was a backlash from the Japanese public. The Japanese looked weak and the Chinese looked like bullies. Japan was not in a mood to do that again.

Of course, the oil and gas, which were there before the fish, are more to the point. They need oil and gas to keep production up and they are pretty much willing to do most anything to keep up with the demand.

Later in 2010, the leaders of the ASEAN Forum, eight of the largest countries in the region, got together with President Obama at lunch in the U.S.A. first. All of them agreed that they needed to speak out about how they were going to resolve disputes, protect commerce at sea, and maintain freedom of navigation and respect for maritime laws in the South China Sea. This was the last thing in the world the Chinese wanted to see. They thought they were making progress on getting the U.S. out of the whole area. Now, we were being invited to come back.

Building Up Strength

If you find it hard to pick up something in your house that is not made in China, then you are not trying hard enough to pick things up, or you took off all those tags that say "Do not remove." I keep this book on a Firelite SmartDisk, run by a MacBook Pro, with a Seagate back-up drive, connected to my Verizon switch and router, all made in China. The lamp, stapler, CDs and telephone that I use on the desk with all of this are also made in China. It actually made me feel better to find out that my printer was made in Malaysia, though that may be because it is old. HP told a person who complained about printers made in China not working well, that all the printers were made in China, Malaysia and Thailand. None were made in the U.S. They did add, "sorry." Of course they may be sorry that all printers are not made in China, or that the Chinese printers did not work. It is hard to tell which.

So, it can come as no surprise to anyone that the U.S. and China do not have trade that is equal, but you are not really seeing the whole story if you just look at the numbers of exports and imports. Equal is not even a close thing there, but in the world of trade, close is measured in millions so the numbers do not look quite so big. It is also fair to say that we are pigs in the world market, according to U.S. Census Bureau figures, which are dutifully updated every month. We spend $500 billion more than we take in, every year. That seems like an impossible number.

If we keep going at rate shown for July 2011, it will be $540 billion, getting close to what we spend on defense. That should scare you.

We trade more with Canada than we do with China, but that is not a good indication of where the problems lie. The amount of trade can be good. What matters is how much we buy from them, and how much they buy from us. Our trade deficit with Canada is not such a big number because we sell them quite a bit. Our deficit with Canada is $3 billion a month and this seems like a big number, because you haven't seen the figures for China yet.

The monthly deficit with China runs about $26 billion. China is half of our deficit total, and that number is fairly consistent over the year. We pay less in interest on the total national debt than China's annual deficit. If you are asking yourself why we allow this to happen, you are probably understanding that this is not a good thing. You would be right.

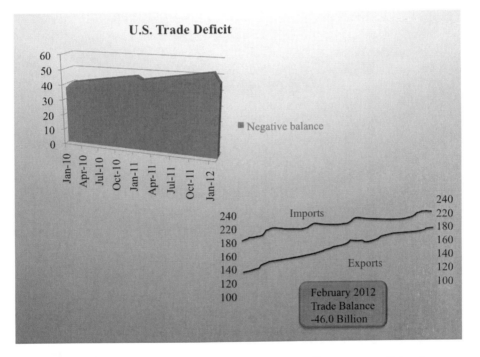

The U.S. trade imbalance allows other countries to influence our politics, but particularly China, which makes up half of the deficit. But, even with no Chinese trade imbalance, the U.S. would still run a deficit (U.S. Department of Commerce).

Normally, what happens when a country runs big deficits, its currency loses value. Countries like China who benefit lose their advantage when their goods become relatively more expensive. If China continually runs huge surpluses with the rest of world — no, it isn't just with us — then their currency should go up in value. That also makes their goods more expensive. Our currency value is not going down and theirs is not going up, defying the rules of economics, at least as I understand them.

The reason that happened, according to the learned economists of the world, is China controls the value of its currency; they don't let the market do it. This is actually pretty smart, considering the bad things that can happen with markets. Prices go up and down and imports vary from year to year. That doesn't happen in China. They control their economy, and they keep control of the value of their currency. It may not be "natural" to economists, but it sure makes sense to me.

China's currency is about 40 percent undervalued (estimates range from 20 percent to 40 percent with the higher number being used most often), meaning we can spend less and still buy Chinese goods. Since they make everything, that sounds like a good thing. We can save money. But, it goes back to the idea that trade is a difference in what they buy and what we buy, and right now that difference is big. The Obama Administration has tried reasoning with the Chinese to get them to let their currency rise a little, and they have done that, but it is a long way from 40 percent and not nearly what we think they need to do. They have had the chance to label China a "currency manipulator," which is not something I have ever heard anyone called before, but they decided diplomacy is better than name-calling. This has led some people in the Senate to introduce a bill to raise taxes on Chinese imports. You can hear the alarm bells from that all the way out to the suburbs where I live. Trade war is what they ring.

Trade wars usually go like this: we start taxing somebody's imports. They start taxing our imports, usually trying for reciprocity, keeping it equal in the impact. There is a little bit of back and forth with adjustments being made but not getting too many goods and services involved for letting the whole reciprocity thing get out of hand. If it goes too far, everyone stops buying everything and we all go into an economy like the one we have now, only worse. Usually neither side wants this, so they try hard not to start a trade war. China is already criticizing the Senate for starting down this road and that criticism is not an idle thing. China has a lever that they haven't pulled just yet. They own a good deal of our debt.

Since China does not have a good way to spend all the money they take in by the exchange of goods — and probably would have a hard time spending it all anyway — they convert it something that is backed by dollars, Treasury bonds. They have about $900 billion of them, and since they are inclined to use third parties to buy into them on their behalf, some estimates go as high as $2 trillion. When the numbers get this high, it is relative. They own a lot of our debt.

This is like the bank that issues my credit card. They own my debt. If they decide to limit my credit, I can try to find someone else to give me another credit card or live with the limit. They can raise my interest rate, establish minimum payments, send me threatening letters when I don't make a minimum payment. They could take it away if things got out of hand. They have leverage from this.

We keep the cost of our debt down by keeping interest rates low. If the demand for debt is low, interest rates will be low. If it goes up, it will cost us more to keep any new debt we have. China buys enough of that debt, that if they stopped, we could have trouble getting other people in the world to buy it all and those costs would go way up. So, if the Obama Administration calls China out on this currency manipulation charge, China can say, "OK, we will stop buying your debt now, and maybe cut trade some too." This would probably not be good for us, and wouldn't do that much on their side to hurt them, even though we are a big customer. President Obama just said it would be better if they didn't do that sort of thing, and the rest of the world was just as unhappy about it as we were. No calling out.

This little high-stakes poker game costs every one of us money, and by some estimates caused the entire jobs crisis we have right now. That reasoning is, the trade deficit represents what China has done to take away jobs, and those jobs would be here if they hadn't done those things. That is a little like saying more people should buy American cars so there might be more employment at GM and Ford. I like my Smart car, which seems to have been made in France, so that will not help the trade deficit with China very much. I have to stop buying things they make for that to work.

I had this choice to make the other day at Home Depot. An extension cord for an electric lawn mower is not something you buy every day. They have gone up in price since I bought the last one 3 years ago. One of them was made in China and cost $32; the other was made in Mexico and cost $82. The one from Mexico had lights on the tips that told a person there was electricity flowing in the cord, and looked thicker and sturdy. I picked up the one from Mexico, and started to walk, but ran into the sales person who was helping someone else. I asked him, "What is the difference between these two?" "What are you using it for?" he asked. "Cutting a small patch of grass with an electric mower." He then bent down and looked at the label on both. He said, "The cheaper one will handle the load the same, and since you don't use it all that often, it will work just as well." Sold.

Andy Grove, who used to be CEO of Intel, said foreign countries don't take those jobs; we give them to them. There is probably more truth to that than the idea that they steal jobs from us. Boards of directors say they can make more money building something in China than in the U.S., and tap into their markets. I would tax them to death for doing that if I could be king.

GE is using that reasoning in sending its Healthcare Global X-Ray Unit to China. They announced a $2 billion program to help the Chinese learn the medical imaging business the GE way. In exchange, they get to tap into that market of potential customers. From a business standpoint, they are right. Their profits go up; their managers get more money. If you believe the 1987 line in *Wall Street* "Greed is good" you can also buy the line that what is good for them is also good for the rest of us. If it were just about greed, we could ignore it.

The fact is, the Chinese make good things that we want, and they make a lot of them. They may not be as careful about safety, healthcare, small business rules, Worker's Comp, and a few other things like that, but the truth of it is, we like what they sell. If the two extension cords were closer in price, I know which one I would have bought. They weren't. Maybe the reason they weren't is a lot more complicated than the thickness of the cables and the lights on the end.

A few of Washington's finest have said, we would be well off, with low unemployment, if it weren't for China's manipulation of currency. When it got down to doing something about that, Congress started introducing some bills to get action. We were going to start adding tariffs to some of their goods. Believe it or not, we do this every now and again and have over the last hundred years. We just don't get the kind of reaction we got this time.

58

Seemingly within minutes of this announcement, *The China Daily* mentioned that China holds a substantial amount of U.S. debt. Of course, the business world already knows this. A Reuters report says they picked up their lobbying efforts with Congress and the Administration to help kill the bill.[10] China can manipulate us to do what they want. That is what war is for.

The comments about our debt are a threat. They appear to be just pointing out the simple fact of ownership, but it means more than just that, and they know it. It is a warning. For several days after, they lowered the price of their currency, a little each day. We knew they could manipulate exchange rates, but now we know they will do it for effect. It doesn't look like much to the casual observer, but there were millions of dollars being made, and lost, in every one of those days. Don't forget that trade deficit. The loss would be ours. A little nudge here and there, with a deficit in the billions adds up pretty fast, and they know it.

The Chinese steal our technology, rack up sales back to us, counterfeit our goods, take our jobs and own a good deal of our debt. They leverage those things to manipulate our business and politics. To those of us in Washington, D.C., it sounds like a normal day at the office. Only, it isn't a normal day, and you are not seeing the whole picture, if you just focus on the economics of relations between the U.S. and China. If you are just focusing on those things, you might miss what is really going on.

3

The Great Wall

The China's *Golden Shield Project* got off the ground in 1999.[1] It is part of a larger effort to build up the capabilities of their bureaucrats to keep an eye on almost everyone in China. It is run by the office that does population control. I have to breathe deep just to think that there is an office of population control there, but that is an internal matter to the Chinese.

There are 12 separate initiatives of the Golden Shield, and like all government projects, they are all running a little behind schedule. They just started quite awhile ago and that part doesn't mean they haven't made any progress. In 2000, the Chinese Communist Party Central Committee organized a meeting with 300 companies, from a dozen or so countries, to talk about building a surveillance network that would combine the national, regional and local police and security agencies to monitor every citizen of China. That is scary.

The Golden Shield is supposed to construct databases of criminal records, fugitives, stolen vehicles, driver's licenses, migration data (that would be human migration, not birds), and a database of every adult in China. It includes Geographic Information Systems, which allow them to geo-locate a building or computer system, closed circuit television, which would see the place, or people located there. With such a system, it is possible to keep pretty close tabs on just about everyone, but surely those who might not be happy with the government. China would say this is an internal matter of no concern to us. I don't think so. Actually, the Chinese would say anything they do is an internal matter to them, but we have to draw some lines somewhere.

The Chinese are quick to do what is called "fragmentation by decomposition." They break down their activities into smaller elements, each one by itself, justifiable in some way. Then they say, for example, "Everyone monitors their populations with cameras" and the people in

Bonn, London, and New York will nod in agreement. They forget that this is a system that is trying to build a database of much more than just camera images, or find fugitives and terrorists by looking at those images. They use this system to keep people in line.

Several cities, like Washington, D.C., have networks of cameras that can monitor the streets and major public areas, but none of them are trying to make a database of every person in the land. They do not target particular groups. If it were just in their own country we would not have much to say about it, but they don't stop there. That is where it becomes a concern to us, and not just an internal Chinese matter.

Control of the Internet

Besides the Golden Shield, the Chinese control the Internet more than most countries would be able to do, by controlling the companies that provide the service and use what they find to change the behavior of individuals. We saw a little of that in the Google filtering. The Chinese wanted to limit anything that smacked of pornography, not just politically sensitive things. The net they were casting was too big for any company to keep up with and one would have to wonder how Baidu could do it any better than Google. Nobody assumes they can.

A user in China cannot access just anything. Twitter, YouTube, Facebook, or the Huffington Post are off limits, and so is anything related to the Chinese dissident groups.[2] If we were to do this, the Democrats could say we were not allowed to visit Republican websites, or anything related to the reform of the government, in any shape or size. We could go to websites of the Catholic church sites that are approved, but those would be limited to the ones controlled by bishops named by our government. We could not visit social websites that were not ours and we would have our own Facebook and Twitter. We could use one browser and it would limit what search results come up. This would be to spare you the hardship of sorting through all those things that could get you in trouble, anyway, so you should find joy in it.

Last year, Baidu had a visit from Chinese propaganda chief Li Changchun and Liu Qi, secretary of the Beijing Municipal Party Committee, "to learn more about the company's business and to give 'important instructions.'"[3] Both officials are members of the Communist Party's

Politburo, which is made up of the party's top 25 leaders. This would be like having two cabinet secretaries visit Google to give them some direction on what they need to do to expand their business. Google might listen attentively, give them some coffee and donuts and send them back to Washington, but Baidu probably would want to pay attention.

The Golden Shield is not something that is strictly used just to keep hackers out, nor to monitor its citizens, but it does anyway. In December 2008, over 300 Chinese citizens posted a document called "Charter '08" which asked nicely for fundamental changes in China's political system. It was signed by another 8000 people before the government shut the website down. One of the group's leaders, activist Liu Xiaobo, is still in jail. So, we could say, you can put anything you want on the Internet in China. Just don't make it political dissent or criticism of the government. They don't allow that, and they have the means to enforce it in ways we can't appreciate in the U.S.

The Chinese control other information that can be troublesome, partly by controlling their press, and feeding the world with their own versions of things. The Russians used to do this all the time too. They rewrote history, on occasion, but modern Russia controls their press as well as China. When one of China's high-speed trains plowed into the back of another one, there were not very many internal reports of it that were not controlled by the Central Propaganda Department. You can read the interpretation of events in Wikipedia and their own press, but once a story is out in the rest of the world, the wire services pick it up and start interviewing people who travel and live in China. Just compare the Wikipedia results with one of the world's wire services and see for yourself.

The Wikipedia report on high-speed trains in China says they lowered the speed of trains after the accident, so fares could be kept low. They have actually modified the Wikipedia report twice since it was originally posted, as more facts emerge that could embarrass anyone reading their version. The truth would have worked just as well, but it would have pointed to the accident and reminded more people of it. Some managers of the train system were relieved of their jobs but they were not relieved because of the accident; they were removed because they were stealing money from the train system. This amazing coincidence occurred for each of the individuals fired over the incident. No mention of the train accident connected to a firing of an official. These are lies that are not even important to most of us. I have trouble trusting people like that.

The *New China Daily* posted these September 2011 extracts from various restrictions placed on reporting of incidents. They are not giving out guidance to young journalism students when they say:

• *Regarding news about the "man executed by firing squad found 'resurrected' nine years later," no re-reporting or reporting is allowed.*
• *All Hunan media outlets are not to hype up the serial murder case in which the killer ate four of his female victims.* From the looks of this one, they must not have tabloid newspapers in China.
• *From the Central Propaganda Department: Regarding the fatal incident on train K256 of the Shanghai Ministry of Railways in which a passenger died after an altercation with crew members, all media outlets are not to conduct independent reports but to wait for the standard copy from the Ministry.*
• *Regarding Zhang Shichao's tortured-to-death case, no reports are allowed for any media outlets.* He had been "helping the police" during a 70-hour interview in his office and died afterwards. His family said he had been tortured.

It would not be hard to imagine what would happen to someone who was hacking into the e-mail or cell phone accounts of some of the senior leaders of China. They could easily find out if anyone was violating the restrictions on censorship. We could say that this is none of our business since they are a sovereign country, and that could be the end of it, but the next time someone points to the superiority of this kind of systems, think about whether it is the kind of place you would want to live. It doesn't seem like the kind of neighborhood that would appeal to me. They deceive their own people.

A War of Information

They control their Internet because that is where information is. Quite a bit of Information War is directed against computer networks, because that is where the information and communications are. This war is about networks, both as vehicles for transport and storage of information. Don't confuse criminals and this type of hacking. They overlap, but criminals are not usually working for a government as much as for themselves. They may have a government customer, if they are stealing something a government wants and will pay for, but they are not exactly government sponsored. Criminals and government hackers use the same techniques, so when they are noticed on the Internet, it is hard to tell the difference. The difference with China is that nobody operates a criminal venture on their networks without them knowing about it. If it is allowed to exist, they know it is there. It is to their benefit to allow criminals to exist as long as they support the overall goals of war.

We have seen network attacks go up dramatically in the last 5 years, but they were going up pretty steadily long before that. We are getting better at seeing this type of thing and that increases the numbers. The difference is in how they are being directed.

The computer attacks are much more "customer oriented" these days because they look for individuals and not just large computer systems. They can be accurate, and narrow, in who and how they target a subject. This type of sophistication is needed because computer penetrations are so successful. There is too much information available, and too many targets. A little more focus helps to reduce the amount of time it takes to get a target that is worth having, and disrupt a user capability or deny that person a chance to act. This is the personalization of war, though it may not be personal to any specific individual, just a person in that position. If I'm attacking the head of NATO, I might not really care who the person is. I just want the office and a way in. This would start with a little look around.

When the Chinese hacked accounts of the McCain and Obama elections teams early in the presidential race, they were apparently looking for position papers that would identify who is writing the kind of stuff the president will read and how they think about these papers. The Chinese keep themselves busy.

They have set up front companies outside China to allow them to influence U.S. elections by contributing money to candidates, without identifying the source of those funds. If you are thinking about SuperPacs getting some of that money, it is not impossible for that to happen. If they hack systems to find out who the leaders are, they can focus their attention. They will ask for favors and exert influence as any other business would. They look like legitimate businesses, and they are trying to influence U.S. policy makers. They can use inside information to do that more efficiently.

This is all part of looking around, identifying people who are influential in political circles, and finding out what policies will likely be enacted. It establishes relationships that can be leveraged for other purposes. It lays out the names of those to be monitored further. You can bet they haven't stopped doing that. This is a long process, but wastes less time than collecting everything from random targets and trying to sort it all out.

China makes it easier by laying out a strategy for electronic warfare that includes rolling their civil and military telecommunications together. It gives them better opportunities for offensive and defensive operations. They seem to be doing the same thing in consolidation of military controlled businesses and commercial businesses, in general. There is really nothing wrong with mixing the two together, except they won't admit they do it. They would prefer we believe their businesses are separate and independent of the state, the army and their intelligence services. I can't blame them. If I knew that bicycle I was about to buy was made by a company owned by the People's Liberation Army, I certainly would give it a second thought. I might even pay more for one that wasn't.

Of the 10 largest exports from China, the big-ticket items are related to networks and computers. Telecommunications equipment is up 25 percent over last year, with China having five of the largest telecommunications companies in the world. Except for ZTE and Huawei, they are mostly for domestic service and nobody else can invest in them. What they have done would be similar to saying to our military, "You and AT&T, Sprint, Comcast, Verizon, eBay, Amazon, and Google will work together to achieve our national defense objectives." We will control all of this from Washington, and we will own stock in the companies that participate. That's not going to happen here.

The British, Indian and Australian intelligence services were said to have told their governments that there were substantial risks from equipment supplied by Huawei. India places limits on what their equipment could be used for.[4] China has complained that India has banned Chinese telecommunications equipment, in violation of the World Trade Organization rules, which China, to hear them tell it, follows very closely.

In July 2010, a *Financial Times* article said Huawei was thinking about buying the network infrastructure piece of Motorola. If you hadn't heard this, it is because it was headed off sooner, in this case, than the purchase of 3Com. This time, Huawei said it was going to use a mitigation agreement that would keep the business side from Chinese influence.

Mitigation agreements are used to keep foreign companies from getting control of companies in the U.S. that have classified work going on. I used to oversee the government side of the first one of these, at Magnavox in Fort Wayne, Indiana. Philips, a Dutch company, was buying them. Magnavox did some classified work in their company and, under rules then, Philips couldn't buy them. To work it out, they came up with a mitigation agreement that put limits on what types of business relationships Philips could have with Magnavox. It was very detailed and very awkward to administer for both of them, as being the first to do anything usually is.

Mitigation agreements rely on two things: both companies follow the agreement, and the buying company does not influence how business is done in the U.S. part of the company. That second part is harder for some to follow, especially if they are losing money, or they have a real board of directors that follows the rules. The U.S. board can stop members from the parent company from attending certain board meetings, and that can cause some hard feelings now and again.

It is partly a "trust me" kind of relationship with the government. It is impossible to oversee every action. Every visit by the management of the foreign firm has to be documented and the business has to be separated so that board members do not get to discuss the U.S. company's business unless they are from the U.S. company. It is hard to enforce and the Chinese know it, but what it also shows is their learning curve is short when they get shut off as they did in 3Com.

Motorola split its company in half and sold the half Huawei was interested in to Nokia Seimens, and filed suit for industrial espionage. It wasn't sour grapes, since this all started in July 2007, before Motorola sold that part of itself. Huawei's next adventure is to try to buy into the LTE (4G) market. That would be the kind of thing my cell phone runs on.

Zhongxing Telecommunication Equipment Corporation (ZTE) and Huawei are involved with the Nigerian mobile telecoms market, mostly through cooperation with existing vendors. Within a few months of Nigerian telecoms being deregulated, they both had offices there. Yes, they also get oil from Nigeria too, so that worked out nicely. In a BBC annual poll on how people in various countries feel about each other,

Nigeria was China's best friend. Almost everyone loved them. I would like to see who was interviewed in that poll. Just as an aside, the Nigerians do not like the U.S. very much.

The combination of China's existing global networks, its communications suppliers, its front companies and army-operated businesses are considerably different than the way we do business in the U.S. These extensions put deep roots in the telecommunications systems of the world and give access to the military to use them. Huawei, as would most companies, denies it has any attachment to the military, which may be accurate, but it cannot prevent the military from using its assets to collect intelligence and do other things too. In August of 2010, eight members of the Senate sent a letter to several senior Obama Administration officials questioning Huawei's equipment sale to Sprint Nextel, asking these officials to respond to their concerns. Congress does not just pick out, at random, any company to complain about, but this letter did not go far enough in identifying where Huawei is making its inroads into the U.S. What they can't get directly, they do by going around our rules.

Yahoo! and Alibaba are business partners, friends so to speak, in that Yahoo! owns 43 percent of the stock in it. Alibaba has tried several times to get them to sell it back, but Yahoo! is not giving it up. A Japanese-based company, Softbank, owns 33 percent. Most businesses consider 5 percent is enough to have some control over how the company operates, and Yahoo and Softbank owned over 75 percent of it.

Baidu, the Chinese Little Google, has announced it was thinking about buying Yahoo!. It is a totally transparent idea to get Alibaba back by buying its stock and, probably someday, Softbank's too. This early warning means the Chinese have learned a little bit about the Committee on Foreign Investments in the United States and how it reacts to unannounced sales. They are giving plenty of warning. Baidu would then own Yahoo! and its stake in Alibaba, All would be right with the world.

Now that Google is out of the picture in China, Baidu will be able to keep a tight hold on search and web activity of the population. Alibaba was probably finding it hard to keep knowledge of any government operations going on in their companies from their two biggest stockholders. If there were any hanky-panky going on, the government would have wanted that cut short, and putting it under another China-based company would do that. It takes a while to do, but it will get done.

Besides upsetting the business world, this shows to what ends the Chinese will go to control their Internet businesses. They had to know this was going to upset some people, and they did it anyway. They don't operate their businesses the same way we do and they don't have the same idea of what the Internet is for. They do not have an open Internet in China, and their businesses are not like ours.

Poly Tech

Eighty-eight Queensway was a set of private companies, but sometimes, even a public company has roots that are suspect. In China, the army owns companies. We might have a hard time understanding this kind of thing, since our army, thank God, does not. Not only does the military own businesses of its own, but they have to operate them for the leaders who manage them, who are military officers and their families. The military families get part of the profits from these ventures. We would not want to try this. It has the potential for corruption, which is exactly what the Chinese have found out.

Poly Technologies was set up by the Equipment Department of the General Staff Department of the People's Liberation Army. At that time it was supposed to be part of the China International Trade and Investment Group, which is the 220th largest company in the world in the Global 500 listings. Its purpose was to export and import military equipment. The president of Poly is He Ping, who is also son-in-law of Deng Xiaoping leader of China until he died in 1997. He Ping retired from the army as a major general after a stint as director of the equipment department.[5] They have something in common with our military-industrial complex and its revolving doors of defense industries. Most of the senior leadership is retired from the senior ranks of the military, or is a direct descendent of someone who is.

Poly has exported defense products, specialized technology, military vehicles, telecommunications, and radar equipment, special purpose instruments and machinery, and chemical industrial machinery. If you go to their website, you can buy gun parts for the AK-47, SKS, and Mauser, which it notes were banned by the Clinton Administration in 1994. Using that logic, this is a sort-of public service.

It does some government-to-government sales through the Bureau of Military Equipment and Technology Cooperation. A Congressional report on missile sales says Poly Technologies was "probably behind the sale of CSS-2 medium-range ballistic missiles to Saudi Arabia in 1987," earning $3 billion to $3.5 billion for the army. Aside from being a lot of money, it must have come as quite a surprise to some countries in the Middle East that the Saudis had medium-range ballistic missiles supplied by China.[6] The Iranians must have loved it. Given the list of things they had been exporting, I kind of wondered how they got into the missile exporting business, since it doesn't seem to fit very well with AK-47 parts or radar equipment.

Like other PLA-owned companies, China Poly Group got into civilian businesses and now gets 80 percent of its profits from civilian companies it owns. This is a little like GSA taking over small companies that supply desk supplies to the U.S. government, or the U.S. Army, with an FBI partner, owning 1000 small businesses. This company has a wide-open business plan. It is hard for us to imagine such an arrangement. A few PLA companies have gotten foreign capital, developed overseas operations, joint ventures, foreign technology, and tax shelters. The tax shelter part of that tells us they have, indeed, learned the way of business. They send their children to U.S. colleges, so they should. Somebody must have missed the classes on lines of business, because those missiles really don't fit with the kind of work they seem to do.

Poly has also become a conglomerate with its own headquarters in Beijing: Poly Plaza, with 24 large businesses that belonged to the PLA and the People's Armed Police (PAP). The police in China actually do some functions done by our Department of Homeland Security. It can be confusing sometimes.

You really have to think about this a little bit to imagine what is going on here. The Chinese military, their intelligence services, and some government agencies do not just do business with their companies. They own and operate them. They make profits and the put those profits into expanding their business areas and maintaining the lifestyle of the rich and famous leaders. They establish real and front companies so they can influence our government leaders to make it easier for them to trade with the U.S. and build up more business. If you get an uncomfortable feeling from this, you are starting to see this unpleasant business for what it is, a new kind of war.

The Plan

Their strategy is called out in a plan. The Chinese system, much like that of the Russians, requires that their government issue a 5-year plan every so often, only this plan is one they actually try to follow. Our 5-year plans usually go out the window about 2 months into them. We don't use them very often and don't follow them as much as we should. They are just "guidelines" for most people.

The Chinese plan their growth. Robert Herbold, Microsoft's former chief operating officer, said when he traveled to China, each place he visited started their briefings with an explanation of what the 5-year plan said, and how it applied to the work they were doing.[7] They tended to focus on three things:

1. improving innovation in the country;
2. making significant improvements in the environmental footprint of China; and
3. continuing to create jobs to employ large numbers of people moving from rural to urban areas.[8]

This causes excitement to all, no doubt. To most of us, this sounds like the State of the Union speech. "I want to have prosperity for all, health care for all, and no tax increases," except that, they start meetings with the plan and they put their money where they need to meet their goals. They are building new cities to grow technology, and modernizing the ones they already have. They make Communism look good. It would be hard to imagine a time in my government career when we started off a meeting with the President's Goals for the Year. Maybe they have something there. Herbold certainly thought so.

Reorganization

In 1998, the military was told to start getting out of businesses — partly because of the corruption — a process supposed to be complete by 2001. This was more smoke. Just remembering that part of the profits from these ventures get fed back into the families of these companies would make a person wonder how that would go. It has been ugly.[9] In 1996 and 1997 two anti-corruption campaigns were directed at the military and the police. In one of the exposed cases, police and customs agents were so heavily involved in smuggling crude oil, they actually were affecting the ability of the state-controlled oil companies to make a profit. Up to a third of the countries' oil was being smuggled. When some of these operations were shut down, tax revenues went up by 40 percent. Three thousand businesses were turned over to local authorities to manage and almost four thousand were closed. Eventually, exceptions had to be made, and besides businesses in railways, civil airlines, and telecommunications, the Poly Group and China United Airlines were at the top of the exceptions list. The army still operates between 8,000 and 10,000 businesses. Along with these changes, they started to reorganize.

Some PLA-run businesses were combined with ones that weren't, producing more confusion that keeps anyone from really telling what parts of industries are owned by the PLA and what parts are not. To add to this confusion, some of the companies are not real companies in the way we normally think of a business.

The FBI, in 2006, said there were 2000 to 3000 front companies being operated in the U.S, some by the PLA, some by Chinese intelligence services. This number is disputed, but the Canadians estimate they have between 300 and 500 operating there.[10] I would really like to see that list of companies that the PLA owns, even if there are only a few, but the wisdom is to classify it. If we tell them we know who they are, it will not take them long to change their name or move, but giving an accurate number would be something they should be able to do so that we all understand the scope of the problem. Not knowing who they are does not help companies that may buy from them.

Front companies are usually set up for a purpose connected with the business the company is in, but they are not very profit oriented. So, if they wanted to get into trading in Alaska oil, they could set up a small company in Alaska and start getting the right people together to make deals. The company doesn't have to make money, directly. It doesn't have to have board meetings or any of those other time-consuming things that are really painful for the officers. They just have to have minutes of those meetings and I can do those up in an hour or so, without bothering anyone. They would invite Alaskan oil businesses to China to discuss exploration and extraction. They can invite trade delegations to visit Alaskan businesses. The trade delegations don't even have to know much about oil, if they have technology related to Alaska, and can spell o-i-l.

They can arrange to visit places where certain types of technology are being used and sold. They follow U.S. trade laws for using "U.S. companies" for certain types of government work. Once they are set up, it gets easier to look like a real business.

A defector from Eastern Europe once told me that if a company looked perfect during an audit, I should spend more time there. He had worked in a front company once and liked it. It was hectic, because they were always trying to be two people at once, the guy who does the hiring and firing of a division, and the guy who is stealing from other business types. It was hard work. To make sure they looked like a real company, they tried to follow every rule of business, especially the rules of a government where they operated.

In 2000, a Justice Department indictment told how this works to siphon off technology. The Chinese have been operating "dozens of companies" with the same purpose, and a few with *only* this purpose. Dozens is not even close to 2000, so I have put that number aside, and just looked at how they do it. I'm more inclined to believe the dozens number and hope the other one is wrong.

A trio of legal U.S. resident aliens were charged with conspiracy to steal trade secrets from Lucent Technologies, a leader in the design of the world's network equipment. The three were working in a joint venture with Datang Telecom Technology Company in Beijing. Datang is a developer of large-capacity switches, optical communications technology, wireless communications systems, full-service access network equipment, telecommunications software, and communication cables. These are all types of network equipment. It is supported by the China Academy of Telecommunications Research, which designs and plans networks, so they all fit nicely together.

The three guys conspired to steal the hardware and software of Path-Star Access Server, which merged analog voice and IP packets from the Internet and handled delivery and routing of them. People who have their telephones and Internet services bundled know the concept.

They set up a front company called ComTriad Technologies, Inc., in January of 2000. It was supposed to be in the business of integrating voice and data over the Internet, which is logical. They were in the process of trying to get private financing from ZiaTech, an Intel Corporation wholly-owned subsidiary, but ZiaTech asked them to show documentation and do a demonstration before they got any money. Any company would. ZiaTech started asking a lot of questions. Since these got really hard to answer, without showing some of the equipment with Lucent's name still on it, they decided better of the financing arrangements. They decided to go to a Chinese company for the money.

Datang, which did see a demo, and maybe missed those Lucent markings, gave them a half a million dollars and formally started a joint venture. Within a year, they may have not been surprised to see that the thieves were starting to put distance between themselves and the newly created company. On the other hand, they may have learned a few things from their business partners.

The thieves took themselves off the ComTriad articles of incorporation and got a post office box to operate from, then took themselves off the Internet registry records of their website, www.comtriad.com, and started using e-mail addresses with no company affiliation. A German real estate company has this website now, so try not to annoy them with calls. They even got cell phones in their wives' names to use for ComTriad business and started using aliases for any public communication about the company. This is not the way officers of a company usually act, but they weren't a real company, so that didn't matter very much. It was obvious they were getting some education on how to run a front company from someone.

By March of 2001, they had transferred the PathStar software to China. By May, the FBI had a search warrant for the website contents and, shortly after, arrested them, getting hardware, drawings and technical documents enough to prove they were stolen. Some of the software being taken belonged to several companies that Lucent paid royalties to. The similarities between Lemko, the company set up by Motorola's employees, and ComTriad should not be lost on anyone. The Chinese seem to have this down to a science. They know how to do it and they have been caught more than a few times.

In February 2011, five people were arrested, including a husband and wife with the surname Liew, in a case that sounds exactly like the others referenced here. The principles in this case were naturalized citizens from China, formed a company and stole secrets from DuPont. They routed those secrets through business deals made with their company and Chinese companies doing the same type of work. The Justice Department says this:

According to the superseding indictment, the government of the PRC identified as a priority the development of chloride-route titanium dioxide (TiO2) production capabilities. TiO2 is a commercially valuable white pigment with numerous uses, including coloring paint, plastics and paper. To achieve that goal, companies controlled by the PRC government, specifically the Pangang Group companies named in the superseding indictment, and employees of those companies conspired and attempted to illegally obtain TiO2 technology that had been developed over many years of research and development by E.I. du Pont de Nemours & Company (DuPont).

Five companies were listed in the indictment.

• Pangang Group Company, Ltd. Pangang Group is a state-owned enterprise controlled by the State-Owned Assets Supervision and Administration Commission of the PRC State Council and located in Sichuan Province, PRC.

• Pangang Group Steel Vanadium & Titanium Company, Ltd. (PGSVTC). PGSVTC is a subsidiary of the Pangang Group.

• Pangang Group Titanium Industry Company, Ltd. Pangang Group Titanium is a subsidiary of PGSVTC and was the entity directly responsible for constructing the 100,000 ton chloride-route TiO2 factory at Chongqing, PRC. Pangang Group Titanium entered into an agreement with USAPTI in 2009 under which USAPTI conveyed DuPont TiO2 technology to Pangang Group Titanium and its employees.

• Pangang Group International Economic & Trading Co. (PIETC). PIETC is a subsidiary of PGSVTC and is responsible for financial matters related to the construction of the Chongqing TiO2 factory. PIETC signed a 2009 agreement with USAPTI under which DuPont technology was transferred.

• USA Performance Technology Inc. (USAPTI). USAPTI is an Oakland, Calif.–based engineering consulting company owned and operated by Walter and Christina Liew. According to the superseding indictment, USAPTI succeeded two other companies owned by the Liews—Performance Group USA and LH Performan — which also were used in the conspiracy to convey DuPont trade secrets to PRC-based companies.

We should get accustomed to this type of case because there have been enough of them for us to know the techniques they are using. Tracking them all down, one case at a time, may not be fast enough to help us defeat them.

Front companies have been around for a long time, but not on this

74

scale. Even 100 of them is more than I want to think about, and I really would like to know who they were. We shouldn't have to guess. Maybe we don't mind trading with them, but it might be better to know that we were buying that baby crib from a Chinese army company. I would like to know, anyway. I really want to know if I am buying software made in China.

In the last few years, they have gotten a little smarter about posting these types of management structures on the Internet. It is harder to trace army involvement in businesses because they have started to use names different from the parent companies and dropped military rank to hide any potential associations. ComTriad obviously knew what to do, once they got with the right people.

We have to see China as a country that is not the same as us, and there is more to it than just the cultural aspects to think about. They are a centrally-managed Communist country with a plan to control as much as they think they need to. They manage business the same way, by using government agencies to develop and operate companies. They pretend to be the same as the rest of the world in how they do that, but they aren't. Combining military, intelligence and business is not usually something any country wants to do, because it puts too much power in the hands of the government. It seems as dangerous as it is.

4

The Borg

Before I was born, President Dwight D. Eisenhower, who had been the Supreme Allied Commander in his previous job, started talking about his concern over the "military-industrial complex," something he saw as needing more control. During World War II, the military and the businesses that supplied goods and services to it had become a little too cozy. They needed to be, but now that the war was over, it was time to start weeding back some of those arrangements. These helped us win the war, but were not needed to keep the peace. He may have had a good idea there. We could use some of that now.

What the Chinese have done is the exact opposite of what Eisenhower was concerned about. They have been winning with the government, military and businesses closely tied together, and they have no intention of separating them. The Chinese have a different focus called People's War.

The People's War is a common thread in their military doctrine, and it has several meanings. Mao saw it as a mix of Army and the people of China, aided by the Communist Party. This is like mixing all together the Pentagon, the general population, and the political parties, which would not work very well in the U.S. They see their economy, military and politics as one thing, done for the benefit of the people. In theory, it is like the Borg in *Star Trek: The Next Generation*, the collective with a goal of world domination, and it is difficult to stop them because they adapt quickly to any new threat.

One of its elements goes back to Sun Tsu, who knew about warfare but, not anything about electronic war. This was before electricity. In the *Art of War*, he said, "All warfare is based on deception. Offer the enemy a bait to lure him, feign disorder to strike him." In their current interpretation, the first goal of this deception is to not be at war.

It recognizes the idea that we all have "red lines" that we will react to when they are crossed. The use of nuclear weapons is one example. We don't like that very much, and are apt to respond accordingly. The concept of red lines is interesting though, because it is used in other types of warfare, especially where it will cause escalation of a battle into something the Chinese might not be ready for. They will fight when the time is right for them, and not when they are best prepared.

David Lai, a professor at the Army War College, teaches students the different perception by playing the Chinese game of wei qi or Go.[1] He contrasts it with chess, which is a Western game that involves a single battle with a goal of capturing a king, and Go that has multiple battles that require the surrounding of territories. Henry Kissinger thought enough of a briefing he got from the professor to describe actions in terms of how China plays the game.

The game uses 361 stones moved onto a grid to get territory. Once they are put on the board, they are not moved around. This allows several places on the board to be engaged at once, so rather than the chess-like battle, there are multiples going on in several places. At the end, (it ends when the players say it is over), the player with the most territories wins.

It is easier to watch how this is done on YouTube than explain it completely. There are a number of videos on different types of circles and tactics to achieve them in these videos. Knowing the tactics can help to defeat them.

Playing a game for 3000 years is not much of a way to predict how someone reacts in war, but it is an indicator of how they might think about conflict. They want to fight in several places at once and they want to use the whole

The Chinese game Go teaches encirclement rather than the direct attacks of chess-like games. The game is not over until the loser surrenders (Wikipedia).

board. They can think about what they want to do in several places at once. This means Information Warfare comes naturally to them.

The People's War sounds like a good thing, everyone working together to overcome obstacles and move along towards greatness. That may depend on which side of the Silk Curtain you sit on. The People have been doing all right for themselves in waging a new war, but they are wired now. That part is new.

Information War has been around for a while, but it was not the same thing 20 years ago. In the middle 1990s when the policies were first published, there were 100,000 websites on the Internet. Today there are 100 million, and none of the top 100 websites were around then. There was no Google, no Facebook or Twitter. At times, I yearn for those days again, just to keep my e-mail down.

There were only about 138 million Internet users in China in 2006 when the U.S. had 210 million. Today, they have twice as many and we don't. But, that isn't all there is to it. Nobody was thinking clearly about what changes the Internet might bring to war, because the Internet was just getting started. Their armies and hacker communities are almost new compared to ours, and they have quite a few new ideas. One of them is how they produce images of war.

Images of War

> China should use nuclear weapons against the United States if the American military intervenes in any conflict over Taiwan. If the Americans draw their missiles and position-guided ammunition on to the target zone on China's territory, I think we will have to respond with nuclear weapons.
> — Maj. Gen. Zhu Chenghu[2]

This is a jolting image of war that is not war. Yes, we can see the mushroom cloud in our mind, children vaporized on the playground, and it is an image that we would not like to see in real life. It is one thing to parade around a J-20 on a runway, and another to talk about a first strike on another country as a part of policy. The Chinese deny that it is official policy of anyone in the senior leadership of government. "We have such a time controlling our generals," they say, hard as that is to believe. Let's hope that now that they have nuclear-armed missiles on their submarines, they can keep a little tighter control of them.

What we do believe, though, is the Chinese would not care if half of their population died in a war like the one described. We say that we would not want to have the kind of casualties that nuclear war would bring, but we still have thousands of nuclear weapons, just in case. If we used a few of them, China would still have twice as many people as we do, although our numbers would drop quite a bit too. It gets out of hand pretty fast.

There could be two totally false assumptions there. First, it would be hard to say that the new China would not care if they had casualties that were half their population. They have jobs and houses and cars and they are growing faster than we are. They may have problems now and again, but not enough to send them to a nuclear war. Second, none of us may be left after a real nuclear war. There are so many rads of radiation floating around that it wouldn't be good for anyone in the world, but least of all to those that were in the fight. We can see what happened around just one nuclear power plant in Japan to get the idea.

In Information War, none of that matters. Truth is not as important as perception. Neither side wants that mutual-suicide kind of war, but the Chinese use the images of war, just like they use images of bad things that can happen to businesses operating in China, to make us think they are willing. They know we believe they wouldn't mind the losses. They do this over and over, with consistent, repeated images, particularly with Taiwan. Donald Rumsfeld says in *Known and Unknown: A Memoir* that when he went to China for a visit, they took him to a public exposition to see a model of swirling fighters and ships ablaze — our ships in Taiwan, with the Chinese attacking them. It wasn't just for him that this was done, but it was nice that he was there to see it.

The most clever of these images are things they don't have very many of, like stealth fighters, submarines, and aircraft carriers. They show us one of a new generation, just one.

Real War

At the same time, we have real concerns with war. China is building up their military in the old-fashioned way.[3] The army has 2.8 million men and women at a time when we are talking about cutting ours back to under a half a million. This isn't exactly a fair comparison, since they lump some functions in the military that we don't. They have a large national police force that isn't included in that number. Officially, their military is used for "local" combat operations, which can be anything they claim as their territory. That's why those lines they draw on maps are important to countries other than Japan and Taiwan. We don't like to see Japan included in the territory that China says it will defend.

Their concept for the use of military force is "Active Defense." Attack only when attacked, but operate offensively. This means that it was OK to throw wood in the water in front of a ship and see what happens, and how far the enemy wants to go. If they attack you for it, it is OK to respond. It may be twisted logic but they can always say they were attacked and responded to the attack. They don't mention the wood in their reporting of it.

They also believe that a response is not bound by time or space, so it does not have to happen right after someone turns on the water hose to get them away from the boat. It is all right to wait, and to strike somewhere else where the enemy is less prepared or does not respond in a way that allows for any kind of force to be used. This doesn't work with training dogs or kids, but it may be different for countries.

The application of force is generally with the army, where increased emphasis and money has come in three places: nuclear offensive forces, space warfare and cyber war. Their offensive nuclear forces are mainly missiles, much like most other militaries of the world, with ICBMs that can reach the entire U.S. Some of them are on ballistic missile submarines. They are trying to build missiles that are more effective against anti-missile systems like those the U.S. has. Now that they have all of our nuclear weapons designs, they can have nice missiles to put them on.

They have a "no first use" policy for military nuclear weapons against other nuclear countries that is a little cloudy. Most countries, like us, just come out with it. "We will not use nuclear weapons first in a conflict." Some of China's military believes first use applies when the country is threatened, nuclear force is threatened by the enemy, or when the other side's conventional forces look to be winning. They also do not see a nuclear weapon detonated in the atmosphere instead of on the ground the same as a first strike. All of this makes it more difficult to figure out what to do in the event they want to go to war.

We certainly don't qualify first use; we say we aren't going to use a nuclear weapon first. The conditions they lay out are things that are not easy to decide, but where national policy is important, we don't like fuzziness. That kind of unclear policy has an effect on everyone else. It kind of leaves their options open, and keeps everyone guessing. It is a deception.

The benefit they get is making other countries hesitant. Keep in mind there are not too many countries in the world with nuclear weapons, so we are not talking about making the rest of the world nervous about it. Just a few countries will be paying attention.

War in Space

China had 15 space launches in 2010, a national record, and they have a program to get something on the moon, whether an explorer or humans. This is the first year that they equaled the U.S. in launches. They have developed anti-satellite weapons and may have intentions of using them against both communications and spy satellites. They practiced by using one on an old Chinese weather satellite, and the U.S. has accused them of using lasers to blind our satellites.[4] They have just launched their fifth GPS satellite, which can mean a number of things, but mostly that they want their own rather than using someone else's. They may just want to have some, if they decide to shoot all the others out of the sky. Branching out into space is relatively new for them, but it is part of the homeland, just higher up.

Our military certainly believes wars will be fought in space. There are commercial, military, and other government interests that go far up into the sky, and if we are going to protect them against other militaries, we need capability there. If they start taking down satellites, we are going to be awfully close to war, but there is a good question about what to do about it. We could respond in kind and knock down one of their satellites, and both of us could end up without any. Our TV and high-priority phone service is going to be limited if that happens, but is it really war? I don't know. We certainly have to think about it because they have shown us they can do it.

The Chinese used business partnerships with Loral and Hughes to obtain technology to improve their ability to launch satellites. Both acted to help China improve its missile launches, and did it knowing they did not have the required licenses to transfer information. As ridiculous as

81

it sounds, a bilateral agreement gave them permission to launch our satellites from launch facilities in China. Who's bright idea was that? Unfortunately for us, "technology controls at the launch sites" were not very good, and the Chinese "probably benefited from access to these satellites."

There is a difference between spying and what happened with Loral and Hughes. When I was still doing industrial security, we had a break-in at one of the facilities I inspected, and a person was found there with his hand in a container that had one of the company's prototype things in it. He was a spy, taking a big chance. Stealing from a company with fences and armed guards is really risky. Instead, the Chinese have access to the object they want to see, and we allow these companies to send the satellites over to them where they can look at them at their leisure. On top of that, Loral and Hughes were helping the Chinese improve their launch success by giving them information they were not allowed to have.

The House Committee report concluded that "U.S. policies relying on corporate self-policing to prevent technology loss have not worked." This falls a little short of understatement. I still have a hard time figuring out why our own government would want to turn our satellites over to another country for any reason. And, just as hard a time figuring out why a company gives information to them that will only make missiles work better that could be targeted against the United States. Both of them were our defense contractors while they were doing it.

The Defense Department used to have a program to inspect defense industries and try to help them maintain some protection standards for information they get from the government. Twenty-two different agencies used that function to keep an eye on their contractors, but it was largely phased out. We need to bring it back and start looking at how this information is being protected when it is given to them. Having that information in computer systems that are in China makes that a very difficult problem to control.

5

Cyberwar

Cyberspace is the area that gets the biggest expansion in the Chinese build-up of defense. It combines elements of regular military and commercial telecommunications companies and uses different types of weapons.

Although Information Warfare has been around for a long time, Cyberwar and Hackerwar are relatively new. I don't believe they are really two things, and neither do very many other people. Computers were not around much before World War II, and did not really get networked around the world until the 1990s. So, when a person says, I have 30 years of experience in Information Warfare, it is always a good idea to ask them what they were doing in the time before networks.

The first time many people in the U.S. were aware of this type of warfare is when they noticed the problems Google had in China. We first heard that they were being asked to filter their search results so that certain types of dissident groups would not show up in the search list. If I did a search of church groups, the Falun Gong would not show up on it. The list of things was pretty long, and Google objected, then, eventually moved to Hong Kong, where they would not have to do that type of filtering. At first, they redirected any mainland China search to Hong Kong, automatically, but they eventually backed off of that, giving their users a choice of service. The Chinese said, "If Google wants to operate here, they have to follow our laws." That was pretty fair by most standards and certainly not war-like in any way. That could have been the end of it, but it wasn't.

Most of the readers of the Google news did not know that the person behind Google in China was a former Microsoft employee, Dr. Kai-Fu Lee. He was born and raised in Taiwan. When Google hired him, Microsoft sued to prevent him from telling anything related to Microsoft, and there was some back and forth on this before it was finally settled.

The good doctor did some of the planning and recruiting for Google, but they had problems operating in China, from the beginning.[1]

Google China had unexplained outages in their website and their chief competitor, Baidu, did not seem to have the same problem. Maybe being in a different city was part of that, but not likely. This is not "fair" in any type of business deals, but the Chinese have not been known for fairness in competition. Google's public relations manager was fired because she gave iPods to senior government officials and billed them to Google. It was acceptable in China to do this, but not in the U.S., so Google fired her and the person who approved the purchase of the iPods.

There was also a running gun battle with the Chinese on web filtering that seemed to be endless and trivial, and it got worse when the Chinese hosted the Olympic Games. They decided it was important to do more filtering and they should filter the Google.com site and the Google.CN site. Google.com was in the U.S. and Google thought this was outrageous. The Chinese did a demonstration of some of the Google search results to show that pornographic material was being displayed by some of the search results. They promised Google would be punished for this. Nobody could have imagined what they might mean by that.

We see Google as the good guys, the guys who Do No Evil. So, in 2010, when China started hacking into Google accounts to try to get access to some information on dissidents, we felt like Google was being treated badly. Google didn't like it either. They crossed one of Google's red lines.

They started looking for people in the U.S. who supported human rights groups in China, and they led them into places we were not happy about. That was when they hacked my Congressman's office. They broke into Google's email accounts called Gmail. Google really didn't like that at all. They said they were going to stop doing filtering of their websites. Everyone there knew what this meant. Dr. Lee decided it was time to leave Google, so he knew what it meant.

The Chinese must find this hard to understand, since the use of their Internet companies to control dissent is accepted national policy. They believe that what they were doing was perfectly acceptable, and should have been recognized that way by the rest of the world. They should have known we were not the same, but they let it get out of hand, when it didn't need to be. Even a little bit of stretching would allow us to accept the idea that they were OK in thinking that it was acceptable to use the Internet to control the population, if they only did it inside China. They didn't do that either.

Most people chalked this up to China looking for dissidents and getting a little out of control with it. This kind of thing happens every once in awhile in places like Myanmar and Tibet, so we should assume it is going to happen and move on. It could easily have ended there, and probably did for most of the people in the world. They stopped thinking about it.

Except ... there is something odd that happens when these type of cases come up. The computer security community starts to look around for similar types of attacks, using the same type of techniques, and looking closer at the amount of damage done in the original. This takes time to do and be accurate. Even a small investigation can take a week, and big ones can take several months. Human beings can forget something important in a day or so, so the hacking of Google was long out of their minds by the time this one was over.

It turns out the good guys were not just getting hacked by people looking for human rights advocates in the U.S. The techniques used to get into the accounts were common in a number of places and it was much more involved than just human rights. They were stealing source code from companies like Adobe, Yahoo!, and Dow Chemical. What kind of source code, we will probably never know because none of them are talking. It turned out 34 companies in all were involved. The more we look, the higher that number gets to be. There is no way this was related to the problems Google was having with the government. It had been going on before any of that started.

Source code is the code that human beings write to lay out instructions for a computer or a network device. It is usually considered more important than the code that comes with the computer because it is the original. All the other comes from it. Source code can be modified and it still looks like the same software running on any of those other computers, but it isn't the same. It may do other things in addition to what it does on my computer or it may not do things it is supposed to. The Chinese can certainly write their own software, so why would they even think about stealing it?

One reason is it takes less time to make your own software if you have source code from somebody else. It cuts the development time down from a year, in the case of a really complicated thing, to a couple of months — or less, depending on the skill of the people doing the work. Let's be clear here, this is illegal, but it does cut down development time. Thousands of lawsuits pockmark the legal landscape of software over just this type of thing.

A second reason is the ability to make software look like the real thing but having it do some things that it wasn't supposed to do. Hackers seem to do this all the time now, though they didn't used to think about it very much. At a simple level, we could modify our mail program to look for "Falun Gong" in an attachment it was sending to someone else, and if it found that name, send a copy to another location without tipping off the user. The possibilities are endless, once you have the source code. By the way, try to find something about the Falun Gong and you will see how successful the Chinese have been on limiting access to anything about them. They have done pretty well.

Now the security community sees that the attacks were not just something limited to the Falun Gong and other dissident groups. Now they want to try to find out where else these folks have been and what they have been looking for. They found more. The techniques were not exactly the same, but they used the same principle. Send a document that has embedded code in it, like a Trojan horse that can take control of a computer, and make it look like something that everyone wants. Hackers used to do this all the time with pictures of naked women or movie stars with clothes on. The subject matters have gotten more sophisticated over the years, but some of the others were more entertaining.

The Chinese were promising things like the new list of military base closures, copies of budgets that had not been released and that type of thing. Although people must have wondered about why they were getting something like this without asking, most of them will open it anyway, believing they should not frown on good fortune. The embedded code executes and the computer is open for the attacker to use.

While the good guys were looking at how this was done, they found something called Ghostnet, a China-based network used for hacking. About all anyone can authoritatively say about this network was in two reports by the *Information Warfare Monitor*, published a year apart.[2]

In the first report, they said they were not so sure that China itself was involved and that the spike in Internet hacking from China could be due just to a 1000 percent increase in Chinese users over the last 8 years. Maybe somebody else did it and the Chinese were being blamed.

Maybe there was a natural explosion in hacking, given the increase in the number of users. All of these are possible. With those kinds of numbers, anything could be behind it.

In their April 2010 analysis, *Shadows in the Cloud*, they had much more on how information was being stolen, what it was, and where it was going. They started looking at an example. The target organization was the Dalai Lama and the information being stolen was coming from Indian embassies in Belgium, Serbia, Germany, Italy, Kuwait, the United States, Zimbabwe, and the High Commissions of India in Cyprus and the U.S. There are probably not a whole lot of hackers in the world who are interested in the Dalai Lama.

The control servers for these attacks were in Chongqing, China, and the Chinese are certainly interested in him. This just happens to be the city that was chosen to install the new Cisco surveillance systems of cameras, part of the Golden Shield for China's population surveillance. The control servers used social networking sites, webmail providers, free service hosting providers, and large companies on the Internet as operating locations and changed them frequently. They used similar, specifically targeted attacks against users, and collected 1500 letters from the Dalai Lama's personal office. They also sucked out the contents of hundreds of e-mail accounts located in 31 different countries. I hate people reading my e-mail, and the friends of the Dalai Lama probably didn't like it either.

They had penetrated enough systems that many of the ones discovered during the analysis done for the second report were compromised during the first attacks but had not been discovered. They had been deep into these systems for a long, long time.

Attribution

The difference in the accountability to China between the two reports was something called *attribution*, the ability to say with reasonable certainty who was behind the hacking. The same thing is true of war. If someone sinks a cruise ship in the Gulf of Mexico, we would like to know where the attack came from and who was behind it.

We want to be able to say who did it, but it isn't so easy to do with hackers. Those who are known find it hard to do much of anything that someone isn't watching. It is always better to not be known, except that other hackers have to know who you are, at least what name you use on the Internet. This is what *personas* are for. It would be possible for the world's hackers to know me as Ian_PoFT, but not by my real name. Ian_PoFT is my persona, and I can make it as elaborate or as simple a person as it needs to be. I can be a young student in high school or a businessman from New Jersey. I can even be a housewife in Atlanta. It takes time to set up accounts and connections so nobody can trace my Internet name back to my real name. That work protects my real identity from my Internet self. There is a little more to it than just that, but close enough.

Hackers are watched by other hackers, people in governments, and private sector companies. Even though there are nearly a billion Internet users, those numbers don't make it impossible to find them. Having someone checking up on everything you do on the Internet is annoying. So, they have to take steps to make sure they don't get caught; or, they cover their tracks so they can deny doing anything wrong. This can go as far as monitoring lines to make sure they are not being traced by service providers, or erasing audit records after they are finished hacking. The ones who have been around awhile are good at this.

One day, one of our analysts found someone coming into our network using a technique we had seen before. We knew he was accessing some data that had been traced from a system that we knew was compromised. We kept dummy accounts on our systems that belonged to nobody. If someone accessed one of those accounts, we knew enough to follow them.

We started to watch this person and develop a profile on him. We had no way of knowing who this person really was, but we had a name and a few Internet addresses that we could work with. It took a few weeks to trace back to his real identity, since he didn't seem to work very hard. When we finally found his location, we knew it was in a country that is normally our friend, coming from a government ministry. We called some of our friends to let them know where this person was coming from.

Just for a moment we had been feeling pretty good about our ability to track someone back to his point of origin, but it didn't last very long. They explained, "If you believe a country ministry is hacking your site, and you were able to trace this person back, then it probably is not someone there doing the hacking." We all knew that was right, but the moment had us feeling too good to think clearly.

Governments that do this sort of thing do not make the kinds of mistakes that allow someone to trace them back. Inexperienced gangs and kids do that. They know about attribution and they know how to avoid it. If all else fails, they want the hackers defense. "It wasn't me; it was someone pretending to be me." They want to create plausible denial. It is a way of life with them because so much of hacking is against the law. It makes perfect sense.

So, while we can say that some type of action was taken by a group or person in China, we will probably never know for sure, unless someone who did it defects to the U.S. and decides to tell us what was going on over there. This happened in 2009, when a person from the Chinese Intelligence Service defected,[3] but it doesn't happen very often. That is a sure way of finding out; the other ways are just educated guessing. Attribution can be an indicator, but there is always some doubt that allows the Chinese to say it wasn't them.

In October of 2011, General Hayden, who used to be director of the National Security Agency and since in charge at CIA for a few years, said the Chinese were part of the persistent threat we face; they were expanding their efforts; we were finding it difficult to stop them from being successful. So, it appears they can deny it all they want. They are doing it, and we already know how. This probably annoyed them quite a bit, but it annoys us just as much.

Living in Bad Neighborhoods

When the Internet started to replace television, we probably should have noticed that it was doing more than that. It was changing the way we interact with each other and, among other things, bringing in people who lived in bad neighborhoods. The Chinese are only some of them, but they are the majority of the new people on the Internet. They don't know how to act, but we are learning that the hard way.

The Internet is usually thought of as a neutral place, not good or bad. This is a myth, that started with a grain of truth, long before the Internet came to be. It was possible to roam around on the computer networks of that day and probably not run into anyone, or anything, that would cause a person grief. It was like a neighborhood where you could leave your doors open at night and people might even come in and walk around the house, but they never took anything or made a mess. There was a kind of strange relationship between the people who owned computers and the people who used them. Mostly, computers were used for good, or from the business side of things, for productivity. Everybody liked that and they felt better about sharing this good for everyone.

By the late '60s, the people who were coming in and walking around started to take things that didn't belong to them. It didn't happen often, but people who operated computers thought it happened often enough that they needed to stop letting everyone in, and started to think about protecting information from anyone who might try to get at it. Some of them were saying "there goes the neighborhood" kinds of things to justify cutting the systems off from each other. Business systems were just connecting to each other for business, but people in those businesses were stealing from each other. A few of them were professional criminals trying to blend in, but not very many. Most of the time, they were just opportunists.

One guy who knew how to program a bank's computers invented a scheme that was pretty clever. He thought that he could slice off a piece of every bank transaction and he could make the piece small enough that nobody would notice. They called that the "salami technique" to make it sound less complicated, but it is not all that easy to do. Still, the money piled up pretty fast, and he got caught, and accounting programs started to round off numbers to eight decimal places — just in case someone tried it again.

Another couple of guys found out that you could go downstairs in an airport and when people upstairs used their American Express to buy checks they could later cash, they could record the electrons that made that happen and play it back to get more of those checks. You don't see those in airports anymore. That is a "playback attack" and we still have some of those around. They just don't always work as well as they did on the first ones. People are pretty smart at thinking of ways to steal money, and nothing we can do will limit their creativity.

The occasional bank VP would use a computer in his office to make phony transfers to companies they had thought up. As it turned out, a few of them went to jail for it, but not all of them. A guy in Ohio, whose name I have long forgotten, was killed in a plane crash and his wife showed up for the funeral; then his other wives showed up. He had five, in all, and five houses, with wives and kids in them all. He was a computer programmer with a legitimate job somewhere, but he wasn't being paid enough to support that many families. These kinds of things still happen, but back then, they didn't happen very often because networks were pretty safe place to go. What there was of an Internet was just a bunch of networks connected together.

In the early '70s, the Air Force started to worry about security of their computer systems, publishing a report called *The Computer Security Technology Planning Study*. It was top secret. James Anderson, who wrote the report, said, "There is little question that contemporary commercially available systems do not provide an adequate defense against malicious threat. Most of these systems are known to have serious design and implementation flaws that can be exploited by individuals with programming access to the system.... The security threat is the demonstrated inability of most contemporary computer systems to provide a sufficiently strong technical defense against a malicious user who is deliberately attempting to penetrate the system for hostile purposes." Today, we could hardly argue with his statement, but things were going to get worse.

IBM had not invented the personal computer, and they had not asked Microsoft for an operating system for it. When they did, anyone with a brain could start playing in my house and we knew this was not going to work out. The neighborhood started changing and lots of people were moving in around us. They didn't look like people I wanted in the kitchen. We had to start cutting back on the number and types of people we let into our networks. In those days, we called it computer security, but it was mostly just cutting off those connections to other systems we were connected to, and being a little more careful about what our people were allowed to do.

Some people in research were talking about connecting up more networks into a giant ball of networks, using the ideas that had come from ARPANET. The computer whizzes thought the more of them they could connect, the better the world would be, but not all of us liked the idea. We needed convincing, so they sent evangelists to talk to us. Everyone on earth could have access to business information that they needed to keep our commerce engine humming along to the next millennium or so, was what they said. We will only have to put data in once and everyone can get to it after that. People can get together and have new ideas flying around like snowflakes. We could all work from home and take care of our kids at the same time. It seemed like a good idea. I liked working from home. They had a convert.

In the early '70s, some ARPANET researchers started talking about computer code that could be used to pass things around from one computer to another without the user being aware of it. There were good reasons for having these kinds of things going on behind the scenes, but there were some bad uses that it might be put to. I remember someone made a Christmas Tree virus that brought up a tree whether you wanted it or not, and that probably didn't go over very well in some of the places it showed up in. We took all that to be good fun, but it didn't last long. It turned out there were some really ugly things that could be done with a virus, including wiping out the data that a user stored on his computer. That was bad, but not nearly as bad as it would get.

The last 20 years have not been very much fun, but the last 10 have been the Nightmare on Elm Street. There are thousands of viruses and worms that can spread without being connected to another computer, and some new ways that would beat virus scanners and security. There are a hundred ways to attack a wireless system, and the more security they try to get, the less effective they seem to be. There is a whole new field of steganography, hiding things in blank spaces of a picture, and variations on the theme. Attacks directed at websites, fake websites, and man-in-the-middle between websites and home computers have taken over. People can come inside my computer, plant a keystroke monitor, and watch it from some place on the other side of the earth. They can see everything I do. I found out a few weeks ago that the vendors built this feature into their smart phones to help them "improve the user experience." I'm sure this is not good, but not many outside of my little world seem to be making a fuss. The newest hacker tools disable the virus software I bought, so it does me little good. Hackers are into the business and government computers I use and stealing things that we should not allow them to have. I can't stop this myself, no matter what I do.

The Internet has spread to a third of the people on earth and not very many of them can do anything about it either. They are just individuals and most of them don't know what people are doing to them. Those that understand it still can't do much about it. The people who are causing this trouble are organized, protected, and really good. They are making it a bad neighborhood. If you think of this as being only a bunch of hackers trolling around on the Internet making money, you would be looking at this the wrong way. The Chinese are using it to undermine our business structure.

Signs of Decay

Most everyone understands what it means to have people around you who do not understand how they are supposed to act. If you go to a bad neighborhood, you can tell without having any signs that say "Warning." One of my Canadian friends asked me to speak in his classroom at the Washington Navy Yard in the 1980s. Since I wasn't from Washington, he said I could take the Metro and walk down. There is a Metro stop there now, but back then, it was five blocks. The Metro stations are pretty nice and there are lots of people around, even at 7 in the morning. They get coffee, pick up a newspaper and chat occasionally about the Redskins, Wizards or the Capitals hockey team.

As I left the Metro station and crossed to go South to the Navy Yard, I passed under a major freeway and it went from pleasant coffee shops and newspaper stands to war zone. Nothing was open; windows were broken in half of the buildings; there was glass on the sidewalks so I was pretty sure the breakage was not that old. It was dark because most of the streetlights were broken. It smelled bad. There was not a soul on the streets anywhere, in any direction I could see. Only a few cars came down the road to the end and they had to dodge glass and miscellaneous rubble, but they did provide some light. I said, "You should not be here" to myself. When you say that to yourself, you have already taken in all the clues and processed them. You don't need a checklist to know it is not a good place.

I stopped at the intersection across from the main gate of the Navy Yard, and a woman was coming across the street towards me. She didn't wait for the walk signal like I did, because she lived downtown where they don't. I said, "Good morning," like we usually did in Richmond. She said, "Are you sure you are in the right place there, son?" I said, "Yes, I'm just going to the Navy Yard, right here." She looked down the street about two blocks and gestured with her head. "The entrance is down there. You can't go in this way. Stay away from those boys on the corner down there and don't be comin' back this way until it gets light." It looked like good advice, and I said, sincerely, "Yes, thank you." I stayed away from the boys on the corner who did not look like they were going to work or school anytime soon, and took a cab back when I was done.

What is hard for us is that some of us live in neighborhoods that have gotten bad over time. They were beautiful when we moved in but they have started to fall down after years of people moving in and out. People who have lived in them for a long time still think they are nice places because they haven't taken a close look.

A bad neighborhood on the Internet is not so easy to identify. You will not be able to say "I shouldn't be here" because it won't be obvious that you shouldn't be. It is a place that starts the behavior that can be identified by discovering and attributing crimes to a source neighborhood, or a collection of them. Attributing means I can say, pretty much for sure, that this address was the place this attack was coming from and not somebody who had taken over that address and was using it in their name. You can see the difficulty there. If I see the Davis Furniture Company attacking me, I can be fairly sure they are not the ones really doing it, unless someone over at Davis has gone off the deep end. It is more likely that the website Davis had his son set up was not quite as safe as he thought and someone captured it. They are just using it to do bad things and Mr. Davis will not know until someone calls him. Even then, he may not know what to do about it, but at least he knows.

People know the place they want to go to by a URL. This show up at the top of your browser, like apples.com, but there are no broken windows or streetlights to let you know that the number it translates to is not a good place to go. The number is an address, unique to that place, but it can be changed faster than moving from one office to another. Some security vendors will sell you a piece of software that will watch these places and tell you to stay away from the ones that are bad. That is a good investment, but hardly foolproof, since they can change them faster than anyone can keep up with. At least, they try.

There is a step in between the typing of a URL and the going to the site that is a translation of that text in the browser to a number. The place this is done is called a Domain Name System (DNS) server. Hackers have taken to attacking these and undermining them so they will send a person to their website which will look like the one you thought you were going to. A normal human being can't tell the difference, so they get sucked into typing their bankcard number and password, thinking they can get a money transfer done. Those software packages that do security are supposed to be able to protect a person from this type of place, but they can only stop what they know about. Criminals and government hackers know what they are doing and try to adapt their sites to stay ahead of the curve.

Most bad guys will put up false road signs to get me to go their neighborhoods. It is directing me to the right when I should be going straight. I have to look closely at the URL to see that it is not what it is supposed to be. If I don't look at it carefully, I will end up in their neighborhood. Once I am there, they can put keystroke loggers on my systems to watch me, steal my credit card info, or my personal data. Then, they can become me. It is a lot like the Stepford Wives, because most people will not know that I am not me anymore. There is more than one me, and there can be hundreds.

Hackers go out of their way to create nice neighborhoods. The Internet is a physical place and a virtual place at the same time, which makes that easier. *Avatar* had the idea right. I can be in a back room in a dive hotel in Kinshasa, but my website shows a stunning crystal front house on a rural mountainside, where only someone rich could live. There are usually children there, and quotes from famous people, inferring this is a great place to buy things. "These unique surroundings provide some of the best investment opportunities a bunch of monks could ever manage for you," they will say. They don't say anything about Kinshasa. They could even be in a government office there and nobody would know.

They can sell pretty photos of naked men and women doing things I had not thought of. This will get my attention and while I am thinking about how it was possible to do that, they can get quite a bit off my computer and plant software besides. A person should really be careful not to go to places like this, but it is not so easy to ignore them, particularly when you are young. Young people are not as afraid of bad things happening to them and they value those lessons from pictures of naked people more than I do.

Bad neighborhoods on the Internet move around quite a bit. Other governments, businesses, and hacker groups like to keep an eye on those places and they set up monitoring to see what they are trying to do and how they are doing it. They produce lists called whitelists and blacklists that indicate how they feel about the different places a person can go out there. Whitelists are places that are allowed and are "good," meaning they are allowed to connect to each other without a lot of questions. Whitelisted places have to keep their systems reasonably secure so they can't be modified to accept bad code from one of the blacklisted sites. The folks who have them don't give them to people like us. Governments keep these to themselves.

Hackers have gotten smarter and can do things now that they didn't know were possible many years ago. They feel good about themselves. Most of the things being done, some government-sponsored people were doing the same thing years ago. The first circuit boards that I remember being modified and replaced in a computer system were put in a casino in the '80s, after slot machines were automated. They paid off more than some of the others, but the guys who did it eventually got caught. Hacks, like modifying memory sticks and leaving them around an office where potential users can find them, are old news in some places. Generations of hackers think they are discovering the newest ways to get in, when they're just rediscovering them. The governments of the world have been doing most of the things hackers do on the Internet since before most of them were born. Only rarely does something new come along.

In 2004, Shadowcrew was one of those. You will not find out very much about this group by wandering around on the Internet except some old stories about two cases. In the first, 19 people were arrested, and 9 others eventually prosecuted. The Justice Department says the indictment charges that the administrators, moderators, vendors and others involved with Shadowcrew conspired to provide stolen credit card numbers and identity documents through the Shadowcrew marketplace. The difference between them and the people who have come before them is they managed to get into the systems that processed credit for companies. They were not stealing one transaction at a time. They were stealing all of them.

The account numbers and other items were sold by approved vendors that had been granted permission to sell. They had to be screened before they could play in this game. In other words, they got vetted by Shadowcrew to be criminals. Shadowcrew members got at least 1.7 million stolen credit card numbers and caused total losses in excess of $4 million. What a person gets prosecuted for is what the government can prove in court. For everything they can prove, there is a good bit more out there. For its time, it was not a big case at all.

One of those arrested pleaded guilty to acquiring 18 million e-mail addresses with associated usernames, passwords, dates of birth, and other personally identifying information — approximately 60,000 of which included first and last name, gender, address, city, state, country and telephone number. There were 4000 users of the closed website that was operated by Shadowcrew. They were selling this information to other people, and most of them were not prosecuted in this case.

Albert Gonzalez worked for the government for awhile as an informant and helped to break that case. But, he was arrested again in 2009, for stealing card numbers from T.J. Maxx, Marshalls, Sports Authority, Target, Barnes and Noble, JC Penny, and 7–11. This time it was 180 million stolen credit, debit, and store card numbers. That is a big number. Now people scramble to buy something that is not a credit or debit card, like my iTunes and Amazon gift cards that can be redeemed online. That way, I can buy things without having a credit card on their computer networks. I know they do the best they can, but that may not be good enough anymore. What Shadowcrew was showing everyone was the inability of the people we buy things from to protect our information, personal data, credit card numbers, e-mails, and other types of things from people who would steal it. The thieves were all over the world, working together, and using the Internet to do it. Shadowcrew is not the only one of these groups either. We are underestimating the amount of harm they do, and overestimating our ability to do anything about it. They can corrupt our ability to use the Internet for commerce and they are protected.

Statistics and Lies

In 2000, there were fewer than 362 million Internet users. In 2010, there were about 2.1 billion. This is almost 1/3 of everyone on earth, so I'm always skeptical of numbers that big. Afghanistan is supposed to have a million Internet users, and that just doesn't seem possible. Go scan around that country on Google Earth and tell me they have that many.

The problem with Internet growth is math. Dr. John Carroll, who was one of the founding fathers of computer security in Canada, used to say there will be some bad people in every group. They will not follow the rules, and some will be destructive or nasty about it. By the same token, there are some really good people out there who will do the right thing, no matter what, even if they lose by doing it. He said there were about 5 percent of people at either end, and the rest of them were scattered on a bell-shaped curve, who are neither good or bad all the time. So, when you increase any population by a significant number, you increase the bad people who can give everyone trouble, and find a few people interested in weird things like cow manure. It is just math. Using the formula, just simple calculations get you to 105 million really bad people out there. The Chinese use this often as a reason for the increased hacking coming from there. "There are bound to be bad people and we will eventually take care of this problem," they say. What they don't tell you is they take the long view of things, and it will not be in your lifetime.

While the number of criminal hackers, and the safety of countries they live in, is increasing, the number of people using the Internet and the things they do there are increasing too. We pay bills, shop, search for knowledge, get service from our governments, communicate, socially network and do business, and the number of those things increases all the time. To hackers, these are called opportunities.

People like to talk to each other, so they enjoy these kinds of places and trust them a little. A Pew Research Center study on social network sites says they have doubled since 2008 and over half of their users are over 35. That was surprising, since we tend to think of these places being for teenagers in high school. It turns out that most teens use the Internet for playing games. I have tried that too, but teens are much faster and more clever than I am. Getting shot every few seconds takes the fun out of it.

About 60 percent of Internet users use at least one social networking site. Their study found that a Facebook user who uses the site multiple times per day is almost as likely than other Internet users, and more than three times as likely as non-internet users, to feel that most people can be trusted. They obviously don't know about the neighborhood.

There are 800 million Facebook users and half of them log in every day. Facebook started in 2004, the same year Gonzalez was arrested the first time. Twitter has 175 million. Linkedin, which is more business oriented, has 34 million users. I dropped out of Linkedin for a while, because too many people were advertising things on it, pretending to be my coworkers and best buddies, but selling real estate in God-knows-where. All the social networking sites have similar problems. Not all of them are crooks, but they aren't my coworkers and people on the same career path, if they are in real estate. Because there are so many people on social networking sites, they make good targets.

Internet sites, good and bad, attract quite a few people. There are about 16.7 billion searches every month, and odds are, someone is going to check out a site if it is out there. Google, alone, does 34,000 searches per second, world-wide. It seems impossible. At least a few of them will want to know why I put up a site for cow manure and will come to it.

If my cow manure site does things it shouldn't, like taking your name and e-mail address book, I will go on the blacklist. The Australian blacklist was posted by Wikileaks and included on-line poker sites, a tourist site, a kennel, and a dentist's office, none of which sounds like a child pornography or sex-for-sale kind of place, but they were doing bad things. What they were doing may be hard to tell by the name, but if you saw the physical location, it would be obvious if the dentist's office was in a part of town where no dentist in his right mind would go. I never underestimate the imaginations of criminals, but using a dentist's office or a kennel for sex, or some other type of criminal thing, does sound odd. The nice thing about the Internet is its ability to let me be all I can be. If I want to operate my sex-for-hire operation from a place that sounds like it could never be one, I can do that.

One reason governments don't like to talk about who is on a blacklist is politics. Sometimes, the people on that list are supposed to be our friends. The Nigerians get some of their sites blacklisted because they have always supported, or neglected to act on, a variety of Internet schemes that collect money from the rest of the planet by dubious means like the "I found a bunch of money and all you have to do to claim is send me $250 as a service fee." They did this before there were computers. Although I hardly feel sorry for anyone who falls for this trick after 35 years of it being used, I don't blame anyone but the Nigerian government for allowing it to have gone on that long. They know who is doing it. They know it is successful. They could stop it tomorrow or the next day with a few raids and a couple of dozen people going to jail. They have branched out into credit card frauds now, so they probably are not anxious to stop any of this.

The Russians have the Russian Business Network (RBN), which is one of the largest and most successful hacker networks in the world. They are best known for child pornography, identity theft, phishing, and computer extortion. Some people don't even see RBN as a criminal organization, because what it does is offer services to criminals who need to use a secure attack base. This makes it all the harder to sort out, since it is like offering a garage to multiple gangs that commit robberies. They put their cars there. They do their planning there. They sort through the money. How much do I know about any of this as the garage owner? I could pretend to be deaf, dumb and blind, like the Pinball Wizard, and know very little, an approach that might be good for my health.

Of course, it is not that simple. My little garage is also renting out the planning functions for robberies, doing some of the preparation of banks to be robbed, laundering money, and providing very safe places to work that cannot be seen or heard by police. The police would have a hard time with my Pinball Wizard story.

When they started to get some heat from the rest of the world, and maybe the Russian government since they have been known to cooperate on rare cases in the past, they moved. They tried to hide behind an Italian front company, but that didn't work, and they pulled the plug on some of their operations until the new side of it could be set up. It should not be a surprise that it was in China. Nobody has seen them since, and talked about it. That says they are good at what they do or they are out of business. Guess which.

These could be isolated examples, but they aren't. One of my professors used to tell us that successful criminals spend as much time at their jobs as you do at yours, and you are not likely to run into one of them that you could recognize. They look normal; they have families and homes; they go to church, sometimes. There are probably more than just the 105 million, because that curve will take in a few hundred million who are just copycats or low-level part-timers; there are a lot of people stealing for a for a living, and some are really good at it. At some point, we wake up and say, "This is a bad neighborhood." Lots of bad things have already happened to us by that time and we don't know about all of them.

About 1 percent of the hackers of the world are really, really good, so we are looking at roughly a hundred thousand of them. Kevin Mitnick, in *Ghost in the Wires*, tells the story of getting birth records from real and dead people and creating drivers licenses, library cards, and records of all kinds, to be someone else. He kept these identities around in case he needed them. He always had to worry that one of those who were still living would notice that someone else was pretending to be him. He monitored his own phone lines to make sure they were not being traced. He used the information systems to make false records of him. There are a few of these kinds of criminals out there and they don't get caught. They have their own very good security and they watch the people watching them. They make websites to communicate and share their methods and results, but they are a really tight group and not very trusting of one another. They don't trust anyone outside.

Most of them who work for governments will never be caught and will go away if discovered. If they are criminals without government support, law enforcement people can eventually track down some of them, but there are still some who never get caught. We tend to measure crime by people who do. It may be years before some of this type of crime starts showing up in the records of credit card companies and government files. We haven't caught up to crime as it is being committed now, and there is always a lag in the time law enforcement takes to get there.

I remember a time when the average bank theft was committed by women 25 to 39 years old. I would have devoted most of my time in banks watching women in that age group, which didn't take much prompting when I was younger. Most major computer crimes were in the millions at that time, but these people were stealing a few hundred and getting caught. They were tellers and they had access to cash, but they were not in the part of the bank where the computers would give them more. The bank's VPs were in those places, and not many of them were getting caught. That slants the numbers toward tellers who are not the ones causing the most harm.

The same thing happens with the Internet. Our law enforcement people catch more criminals in the United States than anywhere else, so it looks like the USA is a criminal haven for Internet crime. China and Russia use those numbers to say, "Clean up your own house before you start complaining about us." They can keep their numbers low by ignoring Internet crime, and that works for them.

Interpol says Internet crime is up to about eight billion dollars a year, though I have seen estimates of $50 billion, so nobody knows for sure. The eight billion number sounds low to me, since there is almost no way to see where someone like the Shadowcrew sold all those numbers to and how they were used by the people who bought them. Some of that is written off as bad debt when it is just crime.

The estimates for theft of businesses' intellectual property are $1 trillion every year. It is a lot of money, and this is the fastest growing form of crime. A good deal of that is government-sponsored theft being paid for by China, but some of it isn't. Sometimes this is business stealing from other business. Sometimes it is spying to find out how a country is doing something that might be dangerous to the rest of us. There is a lot of one type or another going on. It is harder to be caught and prosecuted, which would appeal to folks who don't want to go to jail.

The FBI was recently looking into bids that were made for the World Cup in 2022. I know that seems like a long way off, but the World cup is only held every 4 years, so it comes up faster. There was some evidence that the bids by the U.K. and the U.S. may have been hacked. There are also some allegations that payments were offered to FIFA members (FIFA is similar to a global national football league for those who don't follow soccer), to influence their selection of the site, which went to Qatar. There is nothing new in that. FIFA is always being accused of something like this. This kind of hacking happens every day, so there is not much uncommon about it either. Companies and governments steal bids, estimates, employee names, relative's names, telephone lists, customer lists, designs of products and marketing strategies. The World Cup is not something unique. They do it to try to make a better bid or compete where they can't do very well. They are just trying to get ahead. In most countries it is illegal, but understandable. In some countries it is not illegal and this creates a dilemma for everyone else.

As the Internet Churns

Internet crime was growing before the Internet got to be as big as it is today, but there are some things that make it a more dangerous than it was even 10 years ago. Using the Internet to attack us is part of the national strategies of a growing number of countries. Our new neighbors on the Internet are people we don't get along with very well; they don't know how to act; they are not like us.

The people added to the Internet since 2000 are not North American. That is not an obvious thing to most users of it, since nationality or cultural background does not show up anywhere. If I see a .RU or a .CN after a URL, I know that is Russia or China, but it doesn't say anything about what nationality the person operating the site really is. That just says where the site is registered, not where the operators are physically located. The person who manages the site could be a Latvian on a tourist visa in New York. When RBN went to China, it was looking for a safe place to not be seen.

Most new Internet users are from China, which added 460 million of them over the last 10 years. That is 100 million more than the population of the United States, which might account for the interest U.S. businesses have in getting customers there. We should probably remember that China is not our friend and we are building up our military in the Pacific and cutting it a lot of other places, just to make sure they know how we feel.

A friend of mine lived in China, working for a major company in Europe, and she gave us an example of a culture difference that she noticed in the first week there. She tried driving herself, but only once. On her first day, she came to a railroad track, noticing that a train was coming and most of the people stopped. Some didn't, but that happens everywhere, with people trying to get through before the train got there. But while she was sitting there, she noticed that people were starting to drive up next to her in the lanes that would normally be for cars coming in the other direction. Bicycles and scooters were taking up spaces between the cars. She also noticed they were doing the same thing on the other side of the train. When the train was gone two opposing forces were taking each other on in a game of chicken, all trying to funnel themselves back into normal traffic. She couldn't deal with it and hired a driver.

They are certainly culturally different in many ways, and some of these are important to how they think about the use of the Internet. They are poor. Half of the population lives in cities. They are overcrowded and live in spaces that we would normally call built-in closets. This isn't a crime or a reason for looking down on someone, but it is a reason for being careful. I wonder how people with incomes just over $7000, on average, can afford Internet service. It would have to be close to free there for people to afford it.

103

China is officially atheist. You might ask yourself if religious affiliation has anything to do with our interaction with Chinese on the Internet. Some coworkers of mine went to a country in China's sphere of
influence and they went as missionaries. They told us before they left
that we should never refer to their status in any written correspondence
or e-mail. We should never mention the church that they belong to. We
should always refer to them as teachers. They knew their mail would be
read. They knew the country they were going to was not very tolerant
of Christians. They were going to live in the mountains a long way from
any civilization as we know it. When we started to think about what it
was like to live like this, it made us appreciate living where we do. There
are quite a few countries that could find ways to make a person's life very
unpleasant for something they said on the Internet, and it is not how
most of us want to have to live.

China is always a mystery, but there sure are a lot of people there.
They have tried to use population controls of one child per family that
certainly would not go over very well in most other countries. They go
to great ends to control their population, particularly those who may
not agree with how the government is being run.

India added close to 95 million Internet users over the last 10 years.
India's per capita income is half of China's. They have a billion people
living in a country one-third the size of the U.S. Imagine having the
population of the U.S. double, and have them all living east of the Mis-
sissippi. They average an income like the Appalachian region of the U.S.
The main religion is Hindu.

You can easily see that the Internet is bringing people together who
quite diverse, and while that normally wouldn't matter, there are times
when it does. I grew up in a time when do-gooders like me were going
to school to learn how to eliminate hunger and get world peace by helping
everybody get along. It takes awhile to figure out that people who are
really, really poor are different from middle class America. We called that
the "culture of poverty" to try to sum it all up.

I got to work with social workers while I was in college to see if we
could do some good for our community by helping the poor through
the welfare system in the State of Wisconsin. We found out that some
of the people were homeless; a few of them were drunks who could not
seem to quit drinking no matter what we did; a few could not stop having
children they could not afford; a few were paroles from prison; there

were 12 who were pedophiles and, at first, I didn't even know what that was; a few were out and out thieves who would steal from their own mothers; a few were drug addicts who would steal or sell themselves to other people to get those drugs; a few were really nice people trying to figure out a complicated welfare system. I spent a semester trying to get a woman a refrigerator, and couldn't imagine how anyone could live without one. I knew I was not going to make it in that line of work. The really bad people made it hard, and the system made it awful.

The culture in poverty is different than just being a bad way to live. It influences how people act and how they think. We had alcoholics who were not poor and on the same rehab programs, but they seemed to not get into as much trouble and had lawyers to get themselves out of it. They are mobile and can move away to someplace where nobody knows who they were. They had good jobs with support for their families and good schools for the kids. Poor lives are like a survival run in the desert and this was Madison, Wisconsin, not Chicago, Atlanta or New York City, where it was surely worse. It makes me wonder why anyone in a place like Calcutta would even care about the Internet. These countries are really poor, compared to North Americans who used to be the majority of people on the Internet.

Besides China, some of the biggest Internet user gains for their population size were in Russia, Indonesia, Brazil, Nigeria, Iran, Turkey, Mexico, the Philippines, Vietnam, and Argentina. In a way, the Internet has brought us closer to these people, sort of like cheap air travel, but there are some of these that I don't want to be closer to. I don't use cheap airfares to fly to Russia or Iran either. There is all of the usual benefit of "international understanding" that some will talk about, but the understanding seems to come from us and not them.

Some of them have a history of not behaving on the Internet, or anywhere else for that matter. So besides being poor, they cause trouble. China now leads the world in computer hacking sites and general troublemaking. China, particularly the army, shows up more and more and has become the center of attention for the U.S. intelligence community, because the Chinese have been hacking almost anything that has an Internet connection and stealing everything they can. There are stories on the Chinese hacking U.S. satellites, planting software in our electricity grid, and hacking our defense and businesses at such a rate that they got the attention of the president — who they also hacked during the election.

105

They certainly have been busy, but they are just the newest bully on the block. Russia has done most of the hacking over the past 10 years or so, very similar to what China is doing now.

The one difference with the Chinese is simple. They are hacking everyone in the free world and they don't mind us knowing. They are pretty open about it, but deny everything. I have enemies like this. They will deny, right to my face, something I saw them do. I have recorded evidence. I have my own observations, but they deny it anyway. I switch them over to my own blacklist, which I keep in my head, and I watch them closely after that. I take more notes about what they do, and research them. I never trust people who can lie to my face.

In 1998, hackers were getting into U.S. systems from overseas. They were Russians, and they were into quite few U.S. military systems. They learned from that and got better, and so did we. We just had trouble stopping them. During the Cold War we had some great duels with them and we all got better at playing the game. Nobody got hurt for a long time, but then it all changed in a couple of years and I don't really remember how it happened, but I think it was the gangs.

Russian criminal gangs have operated without much government interference for 20 years. They have developed their own culture and rules, a lot like the old Chicago mobs. A friend of mine helped prosecute one of them and they threatened his children and his wife until she finally divorced him and moved away. That was probably the best thing for her and the kids. Her husband carries a gun every day in his job, but she doesn't. AOL, when it was still going pretty well, hired a security manager who spoke Russian to help them investigate some hackers attacking their customers. They eventually found them and got Russia off of AOL altogether. But, they had already done enough damage to AOL to hurt. Now they don't need AOL because the Internet is growing faster and changing while it grows.

Louis Freed, in *My FBI,* talks about two Russian hackers who were well known in the banking community in the '90s. The first was Vladimir Levin and a merry band of his friends, who managed to steal about $10 million from Citibank customers. Almost all the money was eventually recovered, if $10 million was all they got. Alexey Ivanov was another of the same type, hacking a bank in Los Angeles. Both of these guys were talked into coming to the U.S. and the U.K. to demonstrate their hacking skills for potential employment. Nobody will fall for that trick again, anytime soon.

The Russian Business Network (RBN) is probably the first serious attempt to limit any of them. Maybe the Russians have finally seen the damage it can do to their international reputation and have decided to do something good. Moving hackers to China websites might not be what we had in mind, but at least Russia is no longer seen as the bad guys. The Chinese don't seem to mind it.

Iran is new to the business but has a couple of well-known hackers who have done some good technical attacks against security firms. Iran is not our friend and that leads me to say that they should be watched. Iran and China share a good bit of their networks, and neither of them is our friend. They are probably sharing their hacker knowledge, but it would be hard to prove that one way or another. They are not going to say much about it if they are.

We used to track hackers regularly going through Brazil, so they are either really poor at security down there, or they are allowing it to happen. Maybe both. I have never seen a hacker from Vietnam, though there are some. Vietnam and China went at it in June of 2011 during an argument over some islands that both of them claimed. They hacked each other's websites and tried to do a few other things, but it seemed to die out soon. Neither one of them likes to talk about stuff like that, so there is not much written about the types of attacks that were really being used. Behind those website attacks, there were probably some interesting information warfare things happening too. Both of them are getting good experience, so this is not going to go away.

One of the Shadowcrew was in Argentina, which helped in his prosecution, but I had never heard of a hacker from there until that one. Maybe they are there and just really good, or I haven't been paying enough attention.

Internet users are not just increasing in places with growing populations; they are increasing in countries that don't like us very much. In a BBC survey last year, the Nigerians did not like the USA very much, but loved China. Turkey's and India's opinions towards us are down and were not very high to begin with. This will tend to bias the leadership of those places to tolerate more hacking, and crime, and terrorism directed at us. China helps stir some of that up, and the Nigerians use China to keep the circle going. They not only don't care if one of the little operations in Lagos takes a few million from the retired Americans in North Carolina, they would even laugh about it.

Only a third of Chinese have a favorable view of the United States. This doesn't always mean war, of course, but it is certainly a measure of how predisposed people are to thinking about it. They like Japan even less (71 percent have negative views), and that must give the Japanese quite a bit to think about as the Chinese increase their military missile and combat forces. They are closer to Japan, and some of them remember the Japanese invasion of their country before World War II.

Pakistan could do more damage than any of the rest of them because they have so many inroads into U.S. companies operating in their country and they are not exactly friends of ours. The State Department would probably croak to hear that, but that is the way it is. I would like to know why so many of our credit agencies, medical records, and computer center help desk companies think they can operate from there. These are really, really sensitive operations to have in a country that was keeping Osama safe, helps other groups get nuclear weapons, and loves the Chinese. The only two countries with majorities of negative opinions of the USA were Russia and Pakistan.

We are dragging people online who know next to nothing about computers but want to do things on the Internet anyway. As my engineers used to tell me, you cannot engineer-out "stupid." At least 500 times, companies have put out announcements telling people there was a pfishing attack directed against them. This sort of email has an attachment with the headline "New Company Logo." If you click on this attachment, it will cause your computer to explode and splatter pixels all over you, some other such thing that will be more technical. A normal person would think twice about clicking on that attachment, but some people reading their e-mail are not normal. A few of them will not have read the corporate e-mail since they were on vacation and start with the most current trying to catch up. A few are curious about what pixel splatter actually looks like. A few will think it applies to everyone except those few people in corporate management places where people take care of them. Nothing can happen to these exempt leaders. Those that do click on it will be rewarded with new faith because nothing does happen. Nothing they can see.

Our youth go to those sites in Russia and Eastern Europe that advertise with naked women in various poses of artistic merit. I loaned a computer to one of my neighbor's kids and it came back with a few of these, and loads of other problems that suggested he was going to quite a few parts of the world that are bad neighborhoods. He wasn't old enough to have a credit card to pay for the videos, but I talked to him about how that might work for him when he gets one. He trusted people on the Internet because he didn't know any better. Those engineers didn't know any better either. Besides the other things they were doing, we did catch a few engineers going to sites that had very little artistic merit, and we had one corporate VP selling 2000 images a day from his government-provided computer network. For almost anything a person will do, there is someone who will help them, but there is going to be cost for that.

You have all heard of some of the most common types of computer crime and wonder how any idiot could fall for them. We have the "Note from Your Bank: Please notice that your account is to be transferred to the bank in Grover Island, not later than 27 January 2012. Please verify your account number, password, and expiration date of your debit card by next week so that we can process your new account." Does anyone ask why a bank would ask for such information over the Internet? There are so many of these scams that picking out unique ones is harder than it should be. It is a good profession to get into when there are so many people who will fall for such things.

Epsilon did quite a bit of bulk collection of names and e-mail addresses so they could send out ads and notices to customers of their clients. I know this because I read the news, but also because some of the people like Best Buy, Staples, Verizon, Ritz Carlton and the *Wall Street Journal* have sent me e-mails to say that those addresses were stolen. Somebody has my e-mail from all of these places. Press speculation is that information might be used to craft letters trying to get more information from me, but I stopped looking at these e-mails right away. They can just keep sending the ads out with embedded scripting in them to get access to my system. They think I will still open those attachments. Quite a few people will, because it is too hard to see the difference between one ad and another that looks just like it should.

The folks at Epsilon reported it, but it could have started months earlier. We will probably find out when the congressional hearings start on this. Maybe some of the ads I have been getting were already sent out with those little bits of code embedded in them. Now the hackers know I shop at Best Buy and Staples, stay, now and again, at the Ritz and subscribe to the *Wall Street Journal*. I have already received notice that my subscription needed to be renewed at the *Journal*, and it wasn't the *Journal* telling me that. They can send me letters to make me think my last credit card transaction was kicked back or asking to verify the number because my subscription has lapsed (that actually did happen and ours was not expiring until next year). They can look for credit card numbers and do quite a bit of damage before someone can stop them, depending on how much they are able to collect and correlate.

Which is all the more reason for businesses to do better security with data they keep. Companies like RSA, Lockheed, Northrop Grumman, Target, Sports Authority, BJ's, T.J. Maxx, Stratfor, and hundreds of small businesses all have been hacked. It wasn't a surprise to anyone in computer security.

One of my teams was doing a survey of a small company with venture capital funding. They were going into a new line of business for them, storage of online data for external customers. The venture capital firm hired our company to check out their security before giving them anymore money. It's a good idea.

They basically had no security that would allow them to do business on the Internet. We sent our team out twice because we didn't believe the first set of results. The capital was withheld and the company never went public. It would have taken only a few minutes to get control of that site and all of the information stored there. When companies can't operate on the Internet without losing some of the most sensitive data they have, like customer lists, social security numbers, credit card numbers, and employee information, then they shouldn't be operating on the Internet. But, they still are. This is because businesses see risk differently than we do. If they lose my credit card information, they are only liable for a small amount of the losses that can come from that. I suffer much more than they do. As long as that is true, the burden of risk will always be on the small user and not the companies putting all that information together and losing it.

The Federal Trade Commission estimates there are 8 million cases of identity theft in the U.S. every year, and this is partly where they come from. The crime that results from this is not always visible, since sometimes they don't even know their identity is stolen. The Internet makes it easy and, even advantageous, to be more than one person at once. A person can be 25 people and use the credit cards of all of them in the same day. The companies that lose the information are not the ones paying the bills.

New Internet users are not people of our culture. I don't mean of our nationality, because that isn't enough. These are not Western cultures. That may not matter to some, but it should. There are some really, really bad people on the Internet who peddle child pornography that will make you sick to your stomach, and make those Russians nudes look like children's book material. But, nobody can reach them where they live because they have protection. They sometimes capture videos of what they do to these kids and sell them to make money. There seems to be a never-ending supply of people to buy this stuff, and both sides of those transactions are not the kind of people I want to "like" on Facebook.

China hacks us from multiple places and across business and government targets. They are very successful at both getting in and stealing our secrets. They make the winning bids; they get to compete everywhere in the world. This is the morals of international business newly defined by China. They have managed to make up their own rules and get others to follow them, leaving us with the unpleasant choice of adopting theirs, or standing with our own. I'm for playing by theirs, but it is not as easy thing to do.

There are terrorists on the Internet who can teach a person to make a bomb or tell them how to get chemicals together to make riacin so they can kill lots of people the irony being they sometimes do it for religious reasons. People recruit suicide bombers online, which was against everything I ever thought about suicide bombers being ignorant people growing up in madras someplace in Saudi Arabia, Iran or Pakistan. There are hate groups that would like to eliminate people because they are black, white, Catholic, Muslim, Jewish, or pick your own flavor. Causes of all varieties fight for our souls by trying to intimidate, or lie outright, about what they believe is the truth we should hear. They do this in the name of free speech. This makes people skeptical about the Internet and what they see there — the only good thing that comes of it.

In the countries they live in, the things they do may not even be illegal, or police and courts may be for sale. They abuse women; they kill children because of their sex. I don't like religions that tell me they will kill me if I am not from theirs. These are cultural differences that will not get better with understanding. The Internet is not going to help them.

Crime is just one risk that we face in a bad neighborhood, but this risk is going up pretty fast and the users of the Internet are not taking stock of it. We don't have many measures to say when this risk is too great. I can't decide something like that for myself.

What makes that a dangerous thing to say out loud is our commerce depends on our ability to keep computers secure, and to say there is something wrong with that idea makes businesses on the Internet jump. They don't like anyone saying it. Their customers have to believe it is *reasonably* secure, a term invented by people who were looking at risk at a time when there wasn't very much. What the Chinese are trying to do is undermine the ability to do trade safely on the Internet. They undermine our commerce to make war.

6

Border to Border

Computer systems make their own borders, so we have things going from New York to Los Angeles via Canada, Mexico, or Brazil, so in order to do business, every company deals with other countries' laws, like it or not. When it comes to networks, most companies are international, sometimes without knowing it. It is difficult to think of a large company that has no overseas operations of some sort and companies like IBM, HP, Seimens, McDonald's, China Mobile, Oracle, GM or BAE have thousands of employees in other countries who are directly or indirectly contracted.

All of these have major computer systems and networks that interconnect the world and give them connectivity to their mother ships through those overseas circuits that transport corporate networks. They connect to major business partners, customers, suppliers and their own business units. These change over time; sometimes they grow as they acquire one another; sometimes they go bankrupt and sell off all the assets. Most companies, traditionally, don't like to use the Internet for this kind of thing. They like to separate themselves from it if they can, mainly to protect their internal communications, but they used to be better at it than they are now. We can blame the economy for that, but it would be only partly true.

Businesses are being pressed to find more efficient ways to work because they have competition from places with lower labor rates and cheap currencies, like China. So, they cut staff and try to find cheaper ways to do things. Corporate IT staffs are shrinking and so are their security elements, and there is no way to do all that is needed. One blogger said he had bought security equipment to install, but they were so short of staff they had nobody to install it. They are reducing hardware costs by supporting computers that do not even belong to them, allowing people more leeway in working from home, on their own computers, and connecting a variety of smart phones that can expose their business to greater risks. They shift to wireless office lines because that is also cheaper and can be moved when the lease runs out. And, they outsource to other companies what they can. These all raise risks because they are moving the responsibility for protecting corporate secrets away from the security staff to a user or a partner. At the same time, hackers are targeting more businesses, having more success, and not having to work nearly as hard to do it.

What is hard for most people to see is when this becomes serious to the U.S., as a country. A few hackers hit businesses every day and some of them will swindle some ladies in Arkansas, but that doesn't add up to a national concern. That is because most of us never get to see what the government sees at the top. It gets reports from the CIA on what is going on in the world, reports from National Security Agency on what is happening in the networks of the government, and reports from the business leaders of the major companies in the USA about what is happening to them. This is not security of some data in a computer network. This is national security.

All countries have laws about national security. Just to be clear, they are only worried about their own, not ours. They tell other countries how they are allowed to transmit things through their countries. They spy on the rest of the world to get some more information. They share things with other countries that think like they do and want to share. This is usually considered to be "legitimate self-defense" or some such thing. There are some grey areas here, of course.

Economic warfare is just one of them. Can we steal the bids from the new ship that China wants to build and give them to an ally of ours so they can build it? Can we tell GM and Ford what we know about Chery, the Chinese company that makes automobiles? If a well-meaning person gives us the plans for that new bridge in Kalamazoo can we let our bridge builders see them? In our country the answer is always no. We don't even let our own companies bribe officials in other countries who will not give bids to people who won't bribe them. We could do all of these things, because it is in our power to do it, but it would violate some law somewhere that was written before we became a growing economy in the larger world.

Every country requires access to our computer networks to monitor traffic passing through them, mostly e-mail. They say they will not keep this stuff unless it points to a crime or terrorist activity. They read our mail; they listen to phone conversations. They record a lot they can't listen to and this stuff is stored all over the world in various systems. I remember when East Germany fell and the press started to pour through the Stasi networks of surveillance. People were surprised by how detailed it became and how much information could be collected on almost anyone, if they had the right equipment and the will. There were logs and records on daily conversations and videos to go with them.

Surveillance and monitoring are becoming a science, and most countries are good at it. That is what national security is all about. When the Middle East started to come unglued and there was the collapse of regimes there, the amount and type of surveillance was one of the first things to come to light. The second was the number and types of companies that were making the little boxes that did it.

• Bruce Schneier had a blog article on some equipment from England that could block cell phones in a particular location, intercept them, or get them to transmit codes that were unique to each one that would allow the calls to be traced back to the owner.

• Timothy Karr of the Save the Internet Foundation pointed out that equipment is used in Egypt to monitor names and addresses of people in Facebook, Twitter, and YouTube so people could be watched with greater accuracy. The company that gave them the equipment, he said, was Narus in Sunnyvale, California, formed by some former Israeli intelligence folks. That company belongs to Boeing.

• A Finnish newspaper, *Helsingin Sanomat*, reported that Nokia had sold a "spy network" to Iran that could monitor voice and data, pick out target information and flag it. It can monitor voice, data, instant messages, mobile phones and fixed landlines, e-mail and fax. Nokia says it was a "test system" that could not be used for the fixed Internet. We could only wonder why they would sell them a test system to begin with. What were they supposed to be testing? This is the technology needed in the Golden Shield.

It sounds like a good thing to help out law enforcement, and that kind of logic is what allows the export of these types of things to other countries. What is missing from these license applications to a government is the nature of the crime where the equipment will be used. Speaking out against the Thai emperor can be a crime and 2000 websites were on their blacklist for doing just that. Complaining about the solution the local government has offered to fix that dam may be a crime. The term *honor crime* is certainly not a term that has anything to do with honor. In some countries, if my son decides to marry someone who is not of the same religious sect, she would be killed for it. The people who kill her might be investigated but not arrested. Rape is somehow excused in these kinds of cases and the victim blamed for it. One of the news shows carried an interview with a woman in Afghanistan who had had all of these things happen to her at once and they were going to hang her for the finale. That is not easy to understand.

My son sent me a picture of an airport security checkpoint with a sign that said, "Possession of drugs is Punishable by Death." Americans passing through can certainly see the law is different there. In a stay in Greenland, I got to see how Danes handle drug enforcement. We had a guy come up to our military installation, from Copenhagen, to play the piano. He was a heroin user, which we consider a crime (carrying the things needed to take illegal drugs and possessing them), but we were not under U.S. law there. A storm put him in the position of being out of drugs and no place to go. He turned himself in and asked for methadone. He could have gotten it from the Danes, but the only hospital for 300 miles was the U.S. Military hospital, which didn't carry it. Because he was ill, they put him on the next plane, which was going to the U.S., not Copenhagen, and, on landing, he was arrested for transporting drug paraphernalia. It was justice, but it was hard to tell what kind. The definition of "crime" is different everywhere.

The Chinese like to say that business information of a government owned business is national security information — a state secret. They leave that definition vague and let you figure it out for yourself. That way, if you decide that you want to buy goods from one company but want to find out what the competing prices might be, it will be hard to do. You could be arrested for having that information or using it in the conduct of business. The Chinese are not alone in this kind of thing, but they are at the top of the target list for people who are looking for abuses of it. Ask Rio Tinto, who had several people in jail over it. Since computers save everything, it is not easy to know that you even have some of the things they would call state secrets.

So, every country has an array of equipment that allows them to monitor other countries' people, on the off chance that they may be violating the law. They call this national security monitoring. If you are texting, IM-ing, e-mailing, or are Facebook friends with someone from another country, it is likely you are being monitored somewhere, by somebody, and probably more than just one somebody. This is not spying and it is not illegal in any country that does it. You could be committing a crime you don't know about, or have ever had described to you. Ask Liao Yiwu, who spent four years in Chinese prisons after he wrote a poem called "Massacre" following the 1989 demonstrations at Tiananmen Square. Writing it takes more courage when you know you might be living in prison afterwards.

Moviemakers can show how it is possible to get on a computer and hack almost anything, anywhere, and change information or records, shut down electric grids and open dams to let the flood waters out. Several movies and television shows popularize the myth. If it were that easy, we wouldn't have computers. They would be banned or controlled because they are too dangerous. Our bank accounts would not be safe. Our personal information would be public knowledge. We couldn't use credit cards at all, although I wonder how we do that now, what with all the theft of their numbers. They might even be controlled like guns, registered and have some limits put on who is allowed to have them. Hackers are smart enough to not want that to happen, and so are governments.

I asked a hacker who demonstrated his skills at getting into some of the most secure computers we had why his friends in the hacking world had not brought down most of the Internet. They had the ability to come close to doing that, and we always thought they stopped short. He said, "Because they use it." He was pointing out that bringing it down would have long term consequences that none of them wanted to live with, and would make their job harder. There are more than a few red lines crossed. It would deprive them of some of their best targets and improve the defenses of the rest. Better to leave well enough alone. Better to not make war.

Although we have had some fairly spectacular hacks in the past year, at Sony, Lockheed Martin, and others, the business community depends on the trust we have in their ability to make the Internet safe for commerce. If we start to think it is not safe, Baidu, Alibaba, eBay, Amazon, and Google will not be in business much longer. Hackers are starting to push that limit. If someone wants to undermine the world's economy, that would be a good place to start, but it is more difficult than those movies and TV shows would indicate, and may have the type of unforeseen consequences that hackers know about. Nobody, including the Chinese, want to kill the golden goose, even though it is on life support at the moment.

Starting in November of 2010, several systems were hacked by someone who established over 300 control systems, almost all around Beijing. What made this different was the attackers were going after a place called RSA that was famous for its ability to do encryption of various sorts. RSA makes a token that verifies authorized users through a home network. You would think a place that makes security devices would be secure.

During the next few months, several other major companies were hacked in the same way, only there is a pattern to these that will make anyone who sees the list nervous.[1] There is the IRS, USAA which primarily handles insurance and banking for military people, several locations of COMCAST and Computer Sciences Corporation, a few locations of IBM, the U.S. Cert, which handles investigations into computer incidents at the federal level, the Defense Department Network Information Center, Facebook, Fannie May, Freddie Mac, Kaiser Foundation Health Care System, McAfee Inc — the virus people, Motorola, Wells Fargo Bank (and Wachovia, now owned by Wells Fargo), MIT, University of Nebraska — Lincoln, University of Pittsburg, VMWare, the World Bank, and almost every telecommunications company of any size, anywhere in the world. That last one included all the major telecoms in China. So, they are hacking their own telecoms. It is almost like someone said, "Go out and get everything you can."

There were 760 companies in all, and 20 percent of the Fortune 100. This is the kind of attack, spread over several months and extremely successful, that can get our leaders excited and ready to do something. One of the companies wanted permission from the Feds to go after the people that were behind this and find out where and who they were. That would be nice to know.

There is a breaking point in a relationship with another country that can come without warning or understanding of how we got there, and this is close enough for most people. It is time to do something so the ones who are doing this understand that we cannot have folks hacking into the foundations of the culture we have here. The only thing missing on the list of 760 was churches. It certainly looks like the Chinese did it and, if it wasn't the Chinese doing this, then they need to find out who did, and stop them from operating in their country. It is too much like war for comfort.

What the Chinese have seemingly done is combine their military, academic, and criminal organizations into a more capable bunch of hackers.[2] Then, they complain that they are unable to control this type of hacking by criminal elements, just as the U.S. is unable to control hacking that comes from us. It is just another way of establishing deniability. It is a deception.

They have much more control over what people do and do not do in China than in the U.S.—probably more than any country in the world. When one of their gangs gets caught running drugs or stealing a truck, the guilty don't go to jail for a few years. They get a bullet in the back of the head. In the 1990s, China executed more people than the rest of world's countries combined. During the anti-corruption campaigns of the military-managed businesses, 16 people were executed, to help make the point. That is a little scary.

The Chinese can protest all they want about their inability to control their criminal gangs, but they would be hard-pressed to say they can't control their activities on the Internet. They control everything on the Internet and we don't have to look much further than the Golden Shield to prove it. Their view of the Internet is the opposite of ours.

Intelligence Recon

There is nothing wrong with countries spying on each other, but there are rules associated with it. If you see those CIA folks on television, you would think they were allowed to do most anything, including killing members of our own government to hide the secret society that really runs it. They really can't do those kinds of things without getting in a lot of trouble. Those who don't know the rules, are not spies or have never been involved in spying.

Government spying is very complicated and involves quite a few people. Our government says we spend $80 billion a year doing it, but we can only guess how many there are, since that kind of thing is classified by the government. We won't see the Chinese intelligence budget in print anywhere, but we will see the results. That is probably a better way to judge whether something is working anyway.

If I decide to spy on someone in my neighborhood, there are a number of things I can do. I can research his housing plot and the house itself, the cars that he owns, his trash to see where he works and what he buys. I could mount a camera on my roof and look over his way. This is called "open source" collection because some of the information is not protected by anyone. I might not tell people why I was doing it, or may want to avoid going through his trash while he is still home, so I have to be a little careful about how I go about it. It is really only partially "open" in that sense. I always think about this when I hear that our number one export to China is trash, and 80 percent of discarded computers and cell phones end up there. We do a lot of shredding at our house.

I can also follow him, talk to his the neighbors, his co-workers, his friends at church, or videotape him at various places, though this is not in my nature. This is *stalking* in some circles, so it might also be against the law. I can get a job where he works, or get a job working for him. This is useful if I can stay there awhile and get to know this person. He sees me every day and it is easier to find things out. I can become his friend and visit his family and friends. I can download company information that he has and read things he writes. There is quite a bit that I can find out without going any further in my methods.

If I don't mind doing things that might be criminal to find out more, I can listen to his wireless calls, intercept his e-mail, open his mail or packages, use imaging equipment to observe heat signatures in his house and plant electronic bugs in his cars, his work area and his home. If you are saying, "That isn't very nice," you have discovered the essence of spying. It isn't. Rupert Murdoch can vouch for how people feel about it.

Spying is the collection and analysis of other countries secrets, and it is pretty sophisticated compared to what I can do with my neighbor. It is divided into a number of things called "INTs" that are general categories of capabilities to do things. So, we have a range of other intelligence collection capabilities called COMINT, SIGINT, HUMINT, ELINT, MASINT and the like, that describe a certain type of thing being collected and analyzed. HUMINT, for example, focuses on information that is collected from human sources. Interviewing my neighbors about the house I was interested in would be one form of it. COMINT looks at his communications like his cell phone or computer. Rather than try to figure out all of the different types, it is better just to think about them as spying, using different technologies. These are just ways governments collect raw intelligence. They have a lot more money than people like us.

If I can put all of the government's spying capabilities in my hands for a few days, I might not be able to review all that can be collected before I die. I can have enough information on this guy to write ten books, and then some. Governments have a lot of resources the rest of us don't have and they have rules about how they go about collecting and using information, including sharing it with me. That is not going to happen. Just to be clear, I'm not spying on any of my neighbors either.

The Chinese are good at human intelligence, placing people in a country to work and having them check in every now and again, but not spying on anyone until they are needed. Let's take the case of Dongfan "Greg" Chung, a naturalized U.S. citizen who had been in the country for 40 years. He got caught spying for China because another engineer, working for a different company, was caught and the FBI started watching his Chinese handler. "Greg" worked for Boeing and had some Boeing documents in his trash. He had 300,000 documents in his house when he was arrested. He downloaded space shuttle documents in 2002 and had different projects in his stash. His prosecution was under a new 1999 law that made it a crime to steal trade secrets.

It just shows that spying is against the law most of the time, but not all the time. It depends on what country it is, why it is a crime, and how stupid it was. It is hard to keep a really stupid thing, or a case that has to go to court, out of the press. You hear every once in awhile that so and so tried to sell documents to someone in the FBI and you wonder how they could be so dumb. Well, the FBI is not going around saying they are the FBI at times like that, and they don't dress in a suit and tie when they visit this type of person. They dress like the person expects a criminal to look, probably like any of us on a Saturday morning.

This is a little more confusing in China because they have a kind of mobile policy on what is spying and what is criminal. Their laws are more "flexible" in defining what a state secret is and what is a trade secret, as you remember from the way they treated Rio Tinto. They can change the definition of the information to fit the circumstance and the effect they want to have.

Real spying is not war and is done by almost every government in the world. If the Chinese spy on us, they do it with the clear understanding that we spy on them too. Every country spies on the others as much as they can support. In all the world's governments we understand spying and expect it. That won't help you if you are caught spying in the U.S., because it is criminal. Not-war and criminal are not the same thing. It is just one of those little quirks in the way the law works. We don't go to war because someone commits a crime in our country, or when a country spies on us, or we would be at war with every country except Greenland.

National Security and Business Spying

In the last couple of years, there has been quite a bit of testimony at hearings on Capitol Hill about China spying on U.S. business. This is why we needed that law on trade secrets. This is clearly not the kind of spying a majority of governments usually do, but some do it more than others. We don't allow our companies or government officials to bribe anyone in another country for a contract. In some places that is the only way you are going to get a contract. Some countries would think we are foolish, but there you are.

The Chinese have developed an approach to stealing technologies and secrets that is thoughtful and takes a long view. They don't get in a hurry. In the days before the Internet, I interviewed a scientist who traveled extensively to Russia and China because he had an expertise that very few people had. He asked to see me because I was briefing people like him who had high-level security clearances and traveled to countries where people might want that information. He thought these briefings were effective, but did not achieve the right result. He put it this way: "Dennis, if you tell people there is a Russian under every bush, when they get to a place where there are bushes, they will want to look under them. The secret police will see them looking under the bushes and think that is suspicious, so they will follow them. You tell them they might be followed, so they are looking for that to happen, and that makes them look more suspicious. Let me tell you the differences between how information is taken from people in those places, from my own experience." He then went on for over an hour.

The Russian approaches to him were crude and he usually could see them coming. His interpreter would ask him questions that seemed to be from outer space and totally unrelated to the topic of conversation. He was offered a prostitute and a hotel room to take her to, but he declined. He said he was too old to enjoy such a lovely person. He met strangers at the hotel who asked him questions about his reasons for being in Moscow and chatted about his particular technical specialty as if they had been doing it their entire lives. Some of his fellow scientists had large-bodied men following them around, and they didn't seem to know very much about the conference topics. They were there mostly to prevent defections, which went on anyway, but less often when these guys were around. Their presence discouraged much dialog, but at the same time, since they didn't know the subject at all, the scientists could talk about things of mutual interest. Both the scientists and the KGB knew the game and how to play their part in it.

On the other hand, he attended conferences with his Russian contemporaries and they would be talking about some obscure area of this technology and they would reach a point where state secrets were involved. He could tell them the topic was a state secret and they would veer away from it. They recognized that some secrets would not be shared between them, but they could still work together.

The Chinese were different. They also supplied him with an interpreter, over a period of several years, the same one. The two of them had an understanding that she was asked to take care of whatever needs he might have. He was pretty sure that included sexual needs, because she had mentioned the possibility — just once. He said she would sometimes get close to him and he felt like there was an attraction between them, but she never made a move out of turn. They had a good relationship and it was business-like, but friendly. That was the way he wanted it to be.

She took him to several universities and conferences where he was asked to speak. At one university, he was asked a question about an area of his work that was a state secret. He said he could not reply. The student almost jumped out of his chair to respond, "Why can you not tell us now? A hundred years from now it will not matter to any of us and we will both have the same information you keep from us now." He said he actually thought about this for along time after, because it was true. He said he could not give out that kind of information and there was murmuring from the audience. He stopped answering questions and left. He never heard that question again from another audience, but he did find out how they were able, years later, to get the information he was protecting.

An associate professor at one of the universities in California where the scientist taught was invited to speak at a conference in Beijing. He was not asked very often and was glad to go. Over 100 people met him at the airport. There were various academics, politicians, and people to handle every detail of his trip. He was invited to a dinner that evening and almost the same number of people attended, toasting American friendship. He was the only American there.

At the conference the next day they asked him all kinds of questions and he did his very best to answer them all. He "talked his head off," was the way he summarized the outcome. They were willing to spend time and resources to find the right people to get the information they needed, but they are creating a culture of spies.

A Buildup to War

Where it relates to national security, China has a number of collection programs that have been successful focusing on classified things like weapons and government programs. This is quite a bit different from stealing things from networked computers, because the people who have this information have better security. They encrypt most everything and compartment the information so not everyone has access to everything. The networks are very restricted. About the only way to get access to secrets like that are to have someone who works at a place with the information steal it. That is the hardest and riskiest spying there is.

The Chinese are not the only ones who steal information from us, but the people getting caught at it are, increasingly, linked to China and not Russia.

One of my professors used to remind us that criminals in jails are not a good measure of the capability of the criminal community at large. Government sponsored attackers will be careful and good at what they do. It is just a reminder that for every one of those people who get caught, there are a few really good ones who rarely do, especially ones who have government protection. They are good and getting better.

The Chinese have been doing the old fashioned kind of spying and that is also increasing at the same pace. The year 1985 was the "Year of the Spy." It was a big year for industrial security because there were so many examples we could tell our students about. One after another, they were identified, went to court, splashed the terrible things they were doing all over the newspapers and magazines, and went to jail. We thought it was wonderful.

Twelve people were prosecuted that year, several more in the years before. I was teaching a course in industrial security in Palo Alto, California, and came downstairs to see press in the lobby of our hotel. A secretary to the president of Systems Control, Inc., down the street from where we were had just been arrested for her part in helping a fellow named James Harper, her husband, steal classified information and sell it to Polish intelligence. We didn't get much press coverage of our courses, so we were all a little startled to see cameras and the director of industrial security for the region setting up to make a public statement. There was an entire row of reporters sitting in the back of the room. Then 1985 was an even bigger year, but it is not even close to what we have had recently, yet very few people are paying attention. There were, since 2008, 57 defendants in different courts, charged with spying for China.[3] In the annuals of spying, 57 federal prosecutions in a 3-year span is a pandemic. It is so many, it is a little hard to believe that more people haven't noticed.

• A former B-2 bomber engineer got 32 years in prison for working with the Chinese to develop parts for a cruise missile. The Justice Department said it was a compromise of "some of our country's most sensitive weapons-related designs."

• A married couple went to jail for exporting parts used in electronic warfare systems to research institutes that manufacture items for the Chinese military.

• In August 2010, Noshir Gowadia was convicted of giving the Chinese classified U.S. defense technology. Gowadia helped to make cruise missiles resistant to detection by infrared missiles.

• In September 2010, Chi Tong Kuok was convicted for conspiracy to illegally export U.S. military encryption technology and smuggle it to Macau and Hong Kong. The technology included encryption, communications, and Global Positioning System (GPS) equipment used by U.S. and NATO forces.

It would be easy to say that everyone spies on each other, but it would not be right to say that the Chinese aren't doing more than their fair share of it. For one thing, for every case we prosecute, there are a few more that are going on that haven't been found. That number of 57 is like a warning that their espionage is way up from what it has been and we are detecting quite a few more cases than we have had in the past. What we are seeing is just a small part of what is probably going on.

In the past 15 years, China has stolen classified details of every major nuclear and neutron bomb the U.S. had in its inventory.[4] They have had ongoing espionage activity at the nuclear laboratories (Los Alamos, Lawrence Livermore, Oak Ridge, and Sandia) that produce and develop the weapons. This allows them to make their weapons smaller and easier to shoot a long way on a missile.

> The United States did not become fully aware of the magnitude of the counter-intelligence problem at the Department of Energy national weapons laboratories until 1995. In 1995 the United States received a classified PRC document that demonstrated that the PRC had obtained U.S. design information on the W-88 warhead and technical information concerning approximately half a dozen other U.S. thermonuclear warheads and associated reentry vehicles.[5]

Among secrets, nuclear weapons secrets are some of the most valuable, and closely guarded, we have. When the Chinese have them, it doesn't speak well for our ability to protect anything from them. If they have those, they have a good deal more too.

China has stolen U.S. missile guidance technology and exported it to other countries like Iran, Pakistan, Syria, Libya and North Korea. It sold medium range missiles to Saudi Arabia and trades extensively with Iran,[6] which is not our best friend after trying to get Mexican drug gangs to hit embassies in Washington, D.C. Although, they did say they didn't do that.

• In February of this year, the *Wall Street Journal* published two stories describing attacks on NASDAQ and U.S. oil companies. In the first, there seems to be little evidence anything was stolen, but there was evidence that someone had been in the systems and poking around. In the case of oil companies, the attack was based in China and stole quite a bit of information that might be valuable to anyone looking for oil or looking to buy oil. I guess they are not getting enough from Iran, Nigeria, Sudan, and Angola and they need more.

• In October, the BBC published a story on a Chinese scientist who became a permanent resident in the U.S. He was working for Dow Agrosciences and stole trade secrets on pesticides, sending then back to China. It may not be a coincidence that the GhostNet *Shadows in the Clouds* hackers were getting into Dow Chemical. They may have known where to look. This is an old trick of real spies who pretend they are going somewhere to live, but are just there to spy. Sometimes they go where they are told, and sometimes they just stay put in one place until there is something worth taking. They have real jobs and look normal. They just spy part-time. You might notice the similarities between this and the one with Boeing. The Chinese are taking a long view when they allow a person to go to the U.S. and spy after they get to be naturalized citizens. That takes at least, five years. Naturalized citizens have the same rights as any other citizen and they can have background investigations and get security clearances. Most of them are not spies.

• Beginning in 2007, the Pentagon's $300 billion Joint Strike Fighter project — the Defense Department's most expensive weapons program ever — was regularly losing its computerized data to China. This is bad because it costs a lot of money to develop an airplane and there is not much point in letting someone else have that work for free. Once China has the designs, they can build their own, or they can figure out how to shoot down the one we are building. Neither of those is good for us.

• This year, the Air Force's and FAA's air traffic control systems were broken into with the Air Force's being tracked to China. This is something every country needs, so it is nice to have. It will go well with all those airplanes they are going to build.

There is a certain amount of risk in any of these types of thefts, but there are ways to reduce that by doing the spying inside in a U.S. business. The other day, I stumbled on a company called Verizon with the <.CN> after it and went to their website to see what Verizon had over there. That site latched hold of my computer and wouldn't let me do anything until I allowed access to my systems. I wouldn't, and had to reformat my hard drive to get them out of my Mac. I didn't know there was a Verizon connected to the China Internet domain, and sent them a note about what happened with their company.

I checked AT&T and found that they had been operating in China for 25 years. Deutsche Telecom is there and is forming a partnership with Huawei to build a cloud infrastructure. There is Ford China, a Sony China, an HP China, a Starbucks and a list of 250 others that is not all of them. We have connections to networks for almost all of our major companies that operate in China and they work two ways. Those employees are employees of Ford and they are in the networks of Ford, having access to what most Ford employees do. There are restrictions on what a person can see in all corporate networks but it is an inside connection that starts all of this, and those are much harder to control than the external ones. They don't have to spy to get information through these channels. These are legitimate businesses.

The countries that do spy on businesses, and share that with their own companies, could go out and collect things off the Internet and nobody would mind that. There is even an "acceptable" range of things that businesses do to spy on each other, what is called business intelligence.

Associations, conferences and trade shows are good places to meet people from the competition. They get to know people and exchange information about the companies who are trying to sell products. There is nothing wrong with this kind of thing and it is expected that any person traveling to a show will bring back any information about a competitor that might come their way. There are usually booths, shows and meetings in hospitality suites where the conversation is always worthwhile and the food and alcohol are free. It is acceptable to send slide briefings and promotional material to other folks who ask to help promote business. A lot of information is left lying around on tables and anyone can have it. We were teaching a course in industrial security in San Francisco when a gentleman "from Taiwan" came into the back of the room and started collecting our course handouts. One of the other instructors stopped him and asked him where he was from and he produced a business card from a shipping company. We took the things back from him and had the hotel security show him out. He may have just wandered in, but it seemed like he knew what he was doing there.

From the contacts made at these functions, some things can develop. We can set up a request for information from some of them, a greater level of detail that is needed to decide whether a product is directly suited to a type of business being looked at. The federal government also issues these if a business takes the time to register and get the notifications. They reply to these and get into conferences where "potential bidders" are invited. Between businesses and government conferences, a person can stay pretty busy and collect quite a bit of information what these various organizations are thinking about for the future.

After this round, we could set up additional meetings with targeted companies and visit the sites where the merchandize is made. Before we get to visit another facility, we are likely to have to sign a non-disclosure agreement. It says we don't disclose any of secrets we will see at the place, to anyone else, even with other people in our company who did not attend. These are usually called "site visits" but they are really just specific sales presentations, focusing on a product a client seems to be interested in. So, the "don't tell anyone else" clause is not taken very seriously. Smaller companies don't ask very many questions of someone requesting this kind of meeting, but the bigger ones want to know that the company is big enough to justify the time and money spent on putting these together. After these are over, we can arrange for technical interchange meetings where very specific technical topics get ironed out. By the time the whole process is over, a good deal of information will be doled out, but it is generally not going to be spying, by any definition. It is more like fact finding.

Now put this in the perspective of a front company or a business which has a role in spying for a particular country and you can see the ability to collect useful things like the names of employees in specific technical specialties, the business structures and where all the offices are, where specific things are made, something about the capitalization of the company and how they seem to be doing in their business. Once we have a little more information about them, they can be invited on official visits to our company in China.

We can set up a joint venture or a trade agreement with various technical companies that we need to buy goods from. We can reverse engineer most any product we get and figure out how it was made and the materials that would be required. We can then cost those materials and compare our costs against theirs. We probably have not violated the laws of either one of our countries while we were doing all of these things, at least to the point of being prosecuted for it.

The Chinese are doing more than that, by following an Information Warfare strategy that is much broader and deeper than just the usual collecting of things. They are stealing from businessmen and computers that are supposed to be protected.

129

They steal quite a lot of proprietary things directly from the contractors, but don't confuse this with cyberwar. It is state-sponsored stealing, which is different. The popular press has confused the two and it is probably worth confusing since it is sometimes hard to say where one starts and the other leaves off.

If I steal information about the internal computer switches at Comcast, I might be doing it to prepare for war; I might have the idea to steal service from them, or both. I might just want their software, which is theft. It really depends on intent — how they expect to use what the attack has provided. It could be collection of information for some intelligence purpose, a criminal intent, or it can be used in some aspect of war. The information is the same. If I collect it, I try to save as many valuable things as I can, without really knowing what might be useful in the future. Everyone ends up keeping a lot they don't ever use.

Businesses are pretty smart about these secret things, and protecting themselves against people stealing information is something they try to do. This is sometimes more complicated than a person might think. There are a few things working against success. National security policies are the first of them.

Research in Motion has recently bumped up against the United Arab Emirates (U.A.E.) and India over how encryption is used to protect commercial e-mail. Blackberry encrypts its e-mail and there is nothing new about protecting business interests with encrypted software. But, there is always a hidden tradeoff in making systems very secure. What RIM does to secure the Blackberry is a series of mechanisms to make its business e-mail reasonably secure against interception or tampering. This seems like a good thing. They think so, anyway.

Most of the time it is, until we have a terrorist or drug dealers using the Blackberry to protect their business interests. The ability to monitor them is a matter of national security.

If the U.A.E. does not like the type of security that RIM does, they can ask them to provide the government with a decryption key, or they can go to the company using the Blackberry, and asked for the data from them. A key, or the data decryption of the e-mail, can be justified on national security grounds. RIM now says it leaves the keys in the hands of its business customers. The key defeats the purpose of encryption, but it illustrates a basic problem for intelligence services and businesses doing security.

It is important for the intelligence communities of the world to be able to get information about what other countries and groups are doing, so the U.A.E. is not alone. There are national interests at stake and terrorists to deal with, but what RIM is involved with is securing business systems. They are trying to make systems secure so businesses can protect trade secrets and operations from thieves, extortionists and others on the Internet trying to make a profit by access to private e-mail. This is a very fast and growing area of business in its own right. People steal information for profit. We certainly could design systems that would be so secure that nobody could get into them. But, there always has to be a balance between the national interest (finding terrorists is just one example) and our business interests (protecting e-mail).

It gets more complicated because the national interests of one country are not always the national interests of everyone else. For some hackers, there is a job opportunity in there. Those in the oil business see all the tricks that are being pulled and they want to know how to stop it, or get in on it, depending on which side they happen to favor. They want to get the information. Businesses try to stop them.

If they all banded together to build entirely bullet-proof computer systems, no hackers could get in for a little while. It would not take them long to discover what these systems were doing to make themselves more secure, and to start looking for ways around it. So, they start figuring out what they have to do to get in. At the same time, they could use the techniques that were making those systems more difficult to get into, to improve their own security. At a country level, it would be an arms race, of sorts. The intelligence services don't like this kind of thing, because it makes their work harder too, and they have a bigger stick. RIM will usually lose out to national security.

When the U.S. complained about China hacking into our systems, China said more hacking comes from the United States than from China to us, and we should stop complaining about what they are doing. You can check this sort of thing on SANS website (http://isc.sans.edu/reports.html) every day, and you will find the Chinese were right, though it is close. They have had days when China had many more than the U.S. but some days it is the other way around. On those, more attacks were coming from the U.S., but nobody is saying where they originated. China was inferring that the systems were in balance, and that the hacking was equally spread across the world; we need to leave them alone.

Attribution is not good enough to prove things one way or another, and they know it.

Hackers try to bounce around from one country to another to prevent someone from figuring out where they actually are. This is harder to do than it sounds because it is work to create accounts that are difficult to trace to their original owner. A series of those are needed to make "hops" that can't be traced to their origin. They would rather have people in China believe they were coming from the U.S., which has more computers they can use to target other systems, than using someplace in Estonia, Greenland or Iceland, where they would be easier to find. It is a complicated game, but we should still be able to find and stop them.

Business Interests

There are business interests in making weapons systems, defending against weapons systems, collecting intelligence, and analyzing it. Every country in the world has competing interests here and they are competing for big money.

People with business interests are prone to act to protect them. The U.S. intelligence program in 2011 cost $80 billion.[7] The business of intelligence is the collection and analysis of other countries' secrets, not the protection of U.S. networks. Its interests, however, have nothing to do with how much it spends on protecting information systems, though a good bit of it depends on keeping secrets. It is not an interest served by having good security in all the computer systems of the world. China would see it the same as any other developed country.

In many cases, RIM being only a simple example, the intelligence agencies of the world do not want, or allow, better security. If they were to build entirely bullet proof computer systems, it would not take people around the world long to discover what these systems were doing to maintain their security and start working on ways to defeat the protection mechanisms. At the same time, they could use the same techniques to improve their own security so nobody could get into their systems. It would be an arms race, of sorts. The intelligence services like status quo.

When the U.S. complained about China hacking into our systems, they were inferring that the systems were in balance and we needed to leave them alone.[8] They were not talking about their Intelligence Services hacking, but hacking in general. We would never know if that were true because every country plays a game. They protect their exploitation capabilities better than their defensive ones, so only the intelligence services and the national leadership have any idea of who is winning. If this were a football game, we would say that the offensive playbook is top secret and the defensive playbook is secret. This makes no sense, but it is still one of the rules of the game. Let's call it tradition. Every country plays the game the same.

In most of the time since the ARPANET developed into an Internet, the Defense Department and its executive agent, the National Security Agency (NSA), has been managing the Federal Enterprise policy for how secrets are to be protected. The Federal (IT) Enterprise is big, with a $75 billion budget.[9] The Department of Defense (DoD) is the biggest part of that. Defense and the Intelligence Community came to manage security policy largely because they have the biggest investment in IT of any part of the Federal Enterprise, and it is computers that have all the classified information. They leverage that as the justification for the Defense Department's management role. If federal agencies only had one policy, it would make sense for defense to make it.

In 1981, Executive Order 12333 put NSA in charge of communications security, which at that time was mostly cryptography.[10] That small mission became larger as more and more of computer systems security was taken over by the defense and intelligence agencies. NSA got most of the work because it is the manager of Signals Intelligence (SIGINT), which really has nothing to do with the defense of secrets. "SIGINT is a category of intelligence that includes transmissions associated with communications, radars, and weapons systems used by our adversaries.... NSA's SIGINT mission is specifically limited to gathering information about international terrorists, as well as about foreign powers, organizations, or persons."

While it may seem a far cry from the stated purpose of signals intelligence, from 1977 to 1987, NSA ran every aspect of Federal Enterprise policy that governed the protection of computers, whether they were national security systems or not. They did a very good job in those days and the bulk of that policy and process is still used in cyber security today.

The major policy junctions fall into three types of government systems, those with Sensitive Compartmented Information (SCI) in them (almost always top secret systems), those with classified information that is not SCI (almost always secret level systems), and those with no classified in them. When NSA was running the policy for classified systems, they didn't have responsibility for SCI. The CIA did.

In general, where SCI is concerned, today policy comes from the Director of National Intelligence. Secret systems get policy mostly from the Committee for National Security Systems (CNSS), run by Defense with NSA as the executive agent. The National Institute of Standards and Technology is supposed to do policy for unclassified systems. That is a little convoluted to write down, but it is really simple.

Where they tend to overlap is in the defense part of the intelligence community, the Defense Intelligence Agency, the National Security Agency, the National Geospatial Intelligence Agency, and the intelligence parts of the military services. These latter agencies are conflicted because they are both military (sometimes referred to as Title 10) and IC (Title 50) agencies. They tend to follow the rules they like from defense or intelligence, and play both of them against one another. This is mostly in fun, of course, but it is entertaining to watch.

The National Institute of Standards and Technology (NIST) is supposed to make policy for unclassified systems and you will hear people refer to the Computer Security Act as the source of that. That isn't what the act was for.

I invited the drafters of the Computer Security Act speak at a conference of the Federal Information Systems Security Educators Association, where I was chairman. We were educators, so we assumed the purpose of the act was to legislate requirements for training of the workforce, which was falling behind the policy of the time (1986). It is often cited as the reason why security education is required. It turned out that the real reason was to get the DoD/NSA out of the unclassified areas and put NIST in charge of those. The education of users was a secondary issue. The framers thought NIST would be a good place because NIST traditionally does guidance documents. Most agencies do not see guidance as policy, and can follow it or not, as they choose. DoD couldn't direct them to follow it unless they were DoD agencies. Unclassified would be an agency matter. Congress can be clever sometimes.

DoD exempted itself from this legislation by declaring its major unclassified networks national security systems. National security systems follow CNSS guidelines made by DoD and NSA. Nothing much changed in DoD, but they were no longer supposed to be making policy for other federal agencies protecting unclassified systems.

Each federal agency then makes its own policies from the policies of the director of National Intelligence, Defense (through the Committee for National Security Systems), and the National Institute of Standards and Technology. It is not as confusing as it sounds, at first, and one of the major reasons the government gives businesses less protection than they need.

Businesses are supposed to be able to cooperate at the national level through the Critical Infrastructure apparatus run by Homeland Security and the White House. They have been trying to get legislation passed for 10 years, without much success, because there are business interests that don't want them to, mainly the software and computer industries.

The federal departments and agencies act like independent countries and not part of the same USA we all know. I remember the general counsel of the Army telling us that we could not do security monitoring of Army networks, even though we owned those networks. Army operated them for us. She said it was a privacy matter. That was a new definition of the privacy we used to know, but eventually, lawyers-to-lawyers, we were able to get this worked out. It is parochial thinking.

There isn't any reason to believe that we can't have one network in the federal government. We might even have one now, but you wouldn't know it. The Comprehensive National Cybersecurity Initiative had, as its first sub-initiative, to "Manage the Federal Enterprise Network (FEN) as a single network enterprise with Trusted Internet Connections." So, the White House, at least at one time, saw the FEN as a single network, separate from the Internet. It may also see it as an entity to be managed, but it if does, it is not apparent. There is no management entity designated. Instead, there is a crowded mix of pretenders.

A recent General Accounting Office (GAO) report found that over 50 organizations (including five advisory committees; six organizations in the Executive Office of the President; 38 executive branch organizations associated with departments, agencies, or intelligence organizations; and three other organizations) are involved in CIP (Critical Infrastructure Protection). Adding in state and local entities would greatly enlarge the total number. As the establishment of the Department of Homeland Security in early 2003 underscores, the organizational structure of CIP — and within it, CIIP — may continue to evolve for quite some time, and the form it eventually takes will determine the extent to which infrastructure protection is singled out from or integrated within other elements of homeland, national, and economic security.[11]

135

In the absence of an appointed manager, the Defense Department becomes the de facto lead because it has most of the resources. Someone should ask the White House if the intent of National Security Presidential Directive 54/Homeland Security Presidential Directive 23 (NSPD-54/HSPD-23) was to put Defense in charge of the Federal Enterprise; Congress would have said it was not. Military control of the policies for the national infrastructure is not what we either want or need. There are national defense aspects where that type of oversight is needed, but policy management does not belong in defense.

Outside of government, where parts of Critical Infrastructure Protection are done, each legal business entity has its own networks that are corporate assets, some almost as big as the Federal Enterprise. Each manufacturing facility, pharmaceutical company, railroad, telecommunications, service provider and software manufacturer has its own. The National Enterprise is made up of the Federal Enterprise and the legal business-owned networks that operate under U.S. law.

At the level just below the National Security Council, the president's Critical Infrastructure Protection Board (CIPB) was supposed to be developing collaborative ways to help defend the National Enterprise, combining both the government interests and the business community. It defined the business side of this as a single infrastructure, with individual sectors using similar security systems. When I was on this board, Richard Clarke was the chairman. Howard Schmidt, the current cyber coordinator, was on it too.

At that time, sectors of the economy were to be treated as like-interest defenders of a component of the enterprise. The sectors were things like financial services, information technology, electric power, telecommunications, chemical, and surface transportation (rail industry). We could argue that these groups have a common interest in protecting parts of the enterprise and they probably have similar issues in security to address, but they are not common in how they did much of anything. Some of the utilities, for example, get power from other countries where they have very little say over how the infrastructure is protected. The same is true for most sectors. The CIP Council, the working body of this group, was heavily influenced by the financial industry, a large percentage of which was banking. It came closer than any of the sectors to understanding itself and its networks.

The financial sector saw its networks as in integral part of its business and had substantial regulation of financial transactions by the Federal Reserve. Very strong computer security policies were a tradition with the financial community. Most of the members agreed to them and favored information exchange about incidents. The financial and information technology sectors were pretty much in agreement that more had to be done to integrate the national infrastructure. In spite of heavy regulation, or maybe because of it, the financial sector has good policies that can be followed and understood by the participants, but this does not make its job any easier.

Richard Clarke had a difficult time getting any of the sectors to collaborate as well as finance and IT. They had much the same difficulty as the Federal Enterprise has with the different agencies acting independently. Part of the problem was the way they saw the threat. The financial sector is closely bound by threat — everyone is after the money, and they are all interconnected through the Federal Reserve. This is a tradition of very strong policies that are enforced, centrally managed, and inspected to be sure members meet a minimum set of requirements.

To some extent, the IT sector is similar because it provides services for commercial companies that outsource their processing and are connected to credit card services. The credit card industry has a similar strong policy but does not have he inspection authority that the financial sector has.

The rest of the community did not seem to act like they have a common threat, even though it was clear that information was being stolen from all of them. Getting an understanding of the threat across sectors meant we had to share information across them, not just among the members of each sector, as was being done.

The important thing that came from this was idea that industry could share information about threats through a series of Information Sharing and Analysis Centers (ISACs), which have largely been unsupported since. Although the government has consistently said these sharing organizations were successful, there was only one operating last year. Most of the ISACs worked, but they had several problems with the government side of the sharing process.

Liability turned out to be the greatest problem. We had difficulty with more than one piece of shared information being inaccurate. In one case, the list of affected vendor models identified as vulnerable was wrong and that particular vendor was, understandably, not very happy about that. I don't think anyone in any of the ISACs or on the committees thought this was a serious matter, but it didn't take long for the lawyers to express their concerns of their client's business reputation in some of their customer sites. The ISACs asked for liability relief so they couldn't be sued over a mistake like this.

For the next year or so the committee tried to get bills introduced, help draft legislation and persuade industry leaders to support legislation to limit liability for exchanges of information that identified vulnerabilities between members of the various ISACs. Sitting in those rooms where the mark-ups were being done was an experience.

There were all kinds of businesses and government interests represented, and it was hard to tell, by looking, whether a person represented a government interest or a business interest. There were bills introduced but none of them ever passed. Most of my associates saw it as the first step in sharing information about software vulnerabilities of software vendors, something many lobbyists did not see as beneficial to their interests. It may seem strange that we could share interests in many respects, but not in identifying and sharing vulnerabilities of some of our members' products. The legislation never passed.

Without liability protection, some of the members started to leave the ISACs. Others went later when economics no longer allowed them to participate. The Federal Enterprise did not act like it was leading anyone. It was only in the last year that legislation was introduced to try this all over again, and it is running into all kinds of resistance.

The third problem with the government leadership was the Defense Department. Although it did not participate in this industry committee, DoD wanted to classify everything that dealt with any incidents that were being shared. What it typically did was accept unclassified reports from industry groups, add something to them that was classified top secret, then distribute any details only to the government, particularly DoD, and a few defense contractors with security clearances. This meant that people who did the initial reporting did not get anything to share from the government, and could not see anything they added to the report. It put the Defense Department and large defense contractors in the lead for cyber security.

The CIPB was eventually dissolved. It couldn't get much done even though it did seem to have the right membership. It needs to be replaced with something that has the power of the National Security Council to work together with industry and government. It's strength was in not being dominated by the military or intelligence community. It could work effectively with both, given national support. We need that type of leadership to come from the National Security Council, where the U.S cybersecurity coordinator manages the cybersecurity office. It is the only place high enough in the government infrastructure to manage the complicated political issues that arise between government and private businesses. Now that it has a chance of being a permanent office, it might even have a better chance of being successful. It needs to have representation from the business community and the Federal Enterprise at very high levels and set policy for the National Enterprise.

Infrastructure Wars, the Other Cyberwar

Cyber War is how the military wishes it could use information, or deny information use, to someone who might be at war with us. I mean, really at war, and not just playing around in the system or trying to make money somewhere. It is the kind of thing where they might want to overthrow our government or kill a bunch of people — that kind of war.

There is more speculation than fact published about it, because in spite of what gets into the press, Cyber War is not something people talk about in public. No country does. When a press report said the Russians attacked some websites in Georgia, just as they were about to invade that little country, everyone could see that was happening. The websites in Georgia went down and millions of people who used those sites knew it, but that is not what cyber war is about.

We actually had quite a bit of press discussion about the ability of Iran to recruit and attack a bank in the U.S. with a "cyber missile." A former director of national intelligence even said that this type of strike would essentially bring down the banking system if it struck just two banks — and he said why that might be difficult to recover from. This seems to be the kind of thing we would not want to tell our friends, let alone our enemies.

Closer to reality is the Obama Administration's consideration of using viruses to attack the radars of Libya's military.[12] A *Wired* report says the Administration considered attacking Libya's radar sites but thought it might take too long to get the plan together and launch it. We don't see much like that in the press ever, and certainly not from any administration in recent memory. The obvious difference between what the Russians did in Georgia and what the *Wired* article is talking about is the military-on-military aspect of it. No country likes to talk about this kind of thing, and no administration should.

We occasionally confuse terrorism and special operations, which are part of war or the preparation for war, which are carried out by military units that are part of the execution arm of governments. These might blow up bridges, knock out power systems, disrupt transportation and assassinate leaders. When these kinds of units are doing the deeds, they are a part of war. If a terrorist group did the same thing, it might not be possible to attribute it to any country. Half of the battle is attribution, and half of that battle is finding out what countries are funding the terrorists. Someone is. We know who funds their special operations. Their government does.

We have a better example in the Stuxnet worm, which has become much more public and has been studied for some time now. It is very complicated as a means of war and is certainly not a war that we understand very well. If crippling the centrifuges in Iran is an act of war, then somebody is at war with Iran. Whether such a thing is an act of war, is debatable. If Israel admitted they set it free, then Israel and Iran could be at war. That would be complicated and they both would have to admit to being at war. So, Israel does not say it did anything, and Iran denies it ever happened. Nobody is at war. This is bizarre, if you think about it long enough.

But all these people pretending to not be at war are just fooling themselves, even though, in that case, for a good reason. Admitting you are at war can cause things to ratchet up to a point of throwing missiles and soldiers at one another and we don't want to do that. On the other hand, we need to recognize that the behavior is like war. Neither the Iranians nor Israelis want to do that. Better to not be at war.

This is what makes Cyberwar so nice for everyone. The Chinese have the perfect denial vehicle at their disposal. It wasn't me; it was all those other people hacking into China's computers and using them to hack into other places. It wasn't me stealing those secrets from Lockheed, Google, and Adobe. We are at peace and we only do espionage that all countries do. They are counting on a reciprocal response.

Shadow War

I was program manager of a development program called SHADOW, an intrusion detection network that started as a thought of how missile defense might be able to do intrusion detection fast enough to find, stop, and maintain the information systems that make up a ballistic missile intercept network that finds and shoots a target before it can reach the United States. Missiles can get there pretty fast, so you don't have much time to fool around.

If we were going to stop a network attack it would have to be able to detect the attack event, identify the root cause, prepare to isolate it, and continue to operate the rest of the network to fire the defending missiles. Most of the systems we had were having difficulty doing this type of thing in less than a few hours. We had to be able to do it much faster than that.

What SHADOW showed us, ten years ago, was something that scared a lot of people, including us. There are some pretty sophisticated people out there mapping our networks, testing various types of penetrations, and leaving behind little evidence that they had been there. They were able to do some interesting things like this:

On Tuesday, a person pings a computer on a network by sending out a brief command, directed towards any computer that might be found at an address that says, "Are you there?" Most computers will reply. On Wed, a person pings a computer on another network in the same subnet. On Thursday, another ping ... and so on. If we did the same kind of thing on a street, each day we would mail a letter to one possible street address in a given series — like on the 400 block of James Avenue we send a letter to 401 and we keep track of the addresses where the mail is returned as "No such address." The second day, we send a similar letter to 400 Bluebell Lane, which is the next street over, and we keep doing this until we have all the street numbers. Electronically, this can go pretty fast, and at the end you would have a map of all the computer addresses of every computer on every network, if none of them were protected from such things.

Nobody does this, of course, unless they are mapping the networks and don't want us to know they are doing it. They ping (or use a variety of other methods to get through firewalls to map inside) infrequently on any single network because anyone seeing this kind of activity on a single network would become suspicious. They were mapping all the systems where we had sensors, from the East Coast to the West.

Next, they would go back and run certain types of "probe" attacks against each system to check to see what types of operating systems were being used. Then they would try certain types of attacks to see if patches for known vulnerabilities had been installed on each one. At he end of all of this, they have a map of the network, what each type of computer is, what it is vulnerable to, and, if they take the time to update this once in awhile, they can attack pretty much anywhere and be successful. What they learned to do was to capture these vulnerable computers, chain them together, and use them to launch attacks against other computers. These people have a lot of time on their hands and they are very, very good at what they do.

It reminds me of something Dr. Parker used to tell us at USC, "Criminals spend as much time at their job as you do at yours." So do Intelligence Services. They were preparing to do successive generations of software builds on their attack software, each with new capabilities to do automated penetration and attacks and to gradually improve their products. We observed them testing but not deploying some software, which means they had capabilities they were not showing to anyone else. We were able to predict and warn certain people in the government that the attacks, which brought down eBay and a few others in February of 2000, were going to occur. We said they would happen in January, based on their previous software development cycle, but they did not keep their schedule up very well over the holidays.

This turned out to be a group of six people who had time on their hands and malice in their hearts. A government can devote far more resources to this type of thing, and they won't all take off for Christmas. The Chinese have already been accused of mapping the electrical grid of the United States,[13] but they are bigger thinkers than just mapping the electrical grid. What they probably have done is map telephone switches, computer networks, electrical systems, emergency management subsystems, transportation systems, banking and financial systems, and government. It is not that hard to do, but it takes time. Somebody has been doing it for 25 years now, and if we round up the usual suspects, China will be in there somewhere. It is something they would do if they are really interested in Information War. They don't even have to use the capability; they do a couple of demonstrations just to let us know that they have them. When they rerouted Internet traffic to China, we should have been paying attention.

For about 18 minutes on April 8, 2010, China Telecom advertised erroneous network traffic routes that instructed U.S. and other foreign Internet traffic to travel through Chinese servers. Other servers around the world quickly adopted these paths, routing all traffic to about 15 percent of the Internet's destinations through servers located in China. This incident affected traffic to and from U.S. government (".gov") and military (".mil") sites, including those for the Senate, the army, the navy, the marine corps, the air force, the office of secretary of Defense, the National Aeronautics and Space Administration, the Department of Commerce, the National Oceanic and Atmospheric Administration, and many others. Certain commercial websites were also affected, such as those for Dell, Yahoo!, Microsoft, and IBM.[14]

Most of it was from our Defense Department, which says there is no reason to believe there was anything to be concerned about. It was probably an accident. This tickles my imagination because it just doesn't seem like something that happens as an accident might. Since it does happen in various parts of the world, on a regular basis, it is possible. It is also possible it was just a practice for something bigger.

The Second Principle of War

The most chilling thing Von Clausewitz said about war is something you have to read more than once to absorb: "for in such things as war, the errors that proceed from a spirit of benevolence are the worst.... This is the way in which the matter must be viewed, and it is even against one's own interest, to turn away from consideration of the real nature of the affair because the horror of its elements excites repugnance."[15]

In other words, war may make you sick to your stomach, but if you are going to fight one, it is better to do it without thinking about how ugly it is, or might become. This is something nice guys do — they turn away from it because it is ugly and vicious and they don't like to do things that are either one. We won't win any wars that way, and we certainly won't win this one.

The Chinese are using a simple strategy to get access to the rest of the world's information and control what they can't get. Their Second Principle of War is to "Own it; don't attack it." It is better to buy into an infrastructure than try to hack into one. You can live inside something you own and don't have to worry about whether someone finds you. You are supposed to be there. With hacking there is always the side of it that is criminal and that can get messy when people are arrested and accusations are made in a public record. Sometimes the people you are hacking are better at hacking than you are. That can get ugly. If you are getting caught hacking and spying, it might be better to try something else with a little less exposure. Buying it is safer.

When the deal between Huawei and 3Com fell through, it didn't take the Chinese long to start working on another purchase that would put them into the U.S. markets for telecommunications. Huawei was already selling equipment for its networks to Cricket, Cox Communications and Clearwire, later bought by Sprint.

Emcore, a New Mexico–based company that sold fiber optic equipment for networks and solar panels, was looking for a partner and found one. This company looks a little like AMSC, that small company making the control gear for wind generators. Emcore was going to sell part of its fiber optics operations to a company with a long name, Tangshan Caofeidian Investment Corporation, in the shortened version. CIFIUS did not approve their filing, either. This Chinese company, unlike most, doesn't have a website. That would make a company suspect anywhere. On its website, Emcore says:

> The withdrawal was made jointly in response to an indication from CFIUS that it has certain regulatory concerns about the transaction as it is currently proposed. EMCORE and TCIC had previously made a joint voluntary filing with CFIUS in connection with their proposed transaction, whereby the Company would sell a sixty percent (60%) interest in its Fiber Optics business (excluding its satellite communications and specialty photonics fiber optics businesses) to TCIC in exchange for $27.75 million in cash, subject to certain adjustments. In response to the indication from CFIUS, EMCORE and TCIC remain willing to explore alternative means of cooperation that would address regulatory concerns and meet the parties' objectives.

That sale was not going through, but that doesn't mean they are not going to keep trying to get the technology another way. They are doing two things here: (1) they are buying themselves market share and (2) they are buying opportunities for China's Information War. They are persistent and they don't quit.

Opportunities, Opportunities

As an Apple user, I have to admit Foxconn makes a good product that I like, but it makes me nervous. In a war, Foxconn has access to almost everything I am on the Internet because they make it. iPhones, motherboards for other computers, iPad and lots of other things too. People who make things have the most access to the internal workings of the product and they can modify that product in ways that would expose the users to hacking that cannot be stopped because it is built-in.

There was a case in Australia where a consultant told some government officials that he had found some devices that had been put into computers and these things would send anything the computer processes to another country. When he posted a picture of it, it was easy to see that it was fake. It had a bright red LED that lit up when the thing was running, and the last thing anyone would do is make the board visible to anyone who opened the computer case. It turned out that this person was later arrested because he was planting the things and finding them too. It kept him employed until they found out what was going on, but they believed his story because it is not so hard to do.

Someone, a little more careful, can build in hacking software or firmware, and do it so they wouldn't get caught. People after ATM and slot machines have done all these things at one time or another to make money. People who gamble seem to have great ideas when it comes to getting into slots, including the first of the known hardware hacks where a complete circuit board was replaced with one the user controlled. Slot machines are just another kind of computer. That was 40 years ago, for you budding hackers, so it is not so easy to do these days. Getting caught in a case like that means going to jail, but this is a little different. When a company intentionally making modifications gets caught, it can be really bad for business.

It has a huge cost in product acceptance. How many iPads would you buy if you found out they were transmitting everything you printed to somewhere in Estonia? If we were to find out that Foxconn was building a back door into every iPhone it made, then would that have an impact on iPhone sales, and on our ability to trust Apple products in general? I trust Apple, but Apple does not build the iPhone. I want to know that those who do build anything I have on my computer network are good guys — or at least neutral.

Lenovo, the world's largest maker of laptop computers, is owned by China, which bought it from IBM. Their computers phone home, periodically, to update software and we don't think very much about this. All computers phone home and all can download most anything. It is a similar type of opportunity. Every major computer manufacturer has some of its computer equipment made in China and Dell has three large manufacturing facilities there. Even some companies building computers in Taiwan have manufacturing in China. If we look at the range of computers and computer equipment made in China, that risk can be bigger than we might like.

The government has taken to calling this the "supply chain problem," but just making computers is not the real problem for the rest of the world. The Chinese make the root components of the networks all of us use, the main parts of the networks interconnected through every country. 3Com was making them too, when Huawei was trying to buy them. If they start putting backdoors and hacker access into those boxes, or they manage the networks they ride on, they can restrict the Internet access we get. It isn't easy to do, unless there is enough scale in the attack. The Chinese sure seem to be building to that scale.

The Internet is not one thing. We don't really notice how it works when we access it because it seems like everything is just right outside our door. That makes it seem simple. Go to the Internet Mapping Project, http://www.cheswick.com/ches/map/, and look at what Bill Cheswick, who has been mapping the Internet forever, shows about the layers of Internet service providers that there are in the world. Verizon is in there somewhere, but it looks so small. There is a maze of service providers that is so big and interconnected that almost any kind of attack won't get anywhere.

But, I want to take you back to a point I make early in the book about all the components the Chinese make.

The Chinese seem to think big, but start slow. It is possible they have already managed to get counterfeit chips into fighter planes in the U.S., and 400 fake routers into our networks.[16] They certainly have fake circuit boards and Wide Area Network Cards.[17] These have been discovered because some of them failed and the owners complained to the people who they thought were making them. With time, they will get better and won't be detected quite so often. They have access to almost every kind of computer component they make. They have crept into this market with fakes of various types, components and whole routers. It will only take them a few years to get those parts working the way they are supposed to. By that time, we have a whole lot of these things in our networks, in places we are going to be sorry about.

There are new kinds of viruses that can redirect my router connection to some that are controlled by whoever is passing this thing around. The Chinese certainly know this exists, or they might have invented it, since they have so many anti-virus efforts going on. What this allows them to do is route traffic to networks they control. Then, they may not have to control all the equipment on the Internet, to have everyone connect to something they own.

With every passing day, they have new opportunities and they are expanding those as fast as they can. In those five network companies the Chinese own, there are circuits all over the world, so they control huge portions of the networks that use them. They supply most of the network components and phones from supplies they make. They have agreements with other companies that give them access to more. What's more, these companies are government-owned. They don't say very much about themselves on the Internet. Most of them are based in Hong Kong and they have no competition. No international companies may compete with them in China, so nobody is going to buy into their networks. When it comes to global infrastructure, the Chinese own a lot of it, and we may not realize how much, or what it means to us.

China Telecom is the oldest and largest of their telecom structure. It is the largest mobile phone company in the world, by number of subscribers, and has the largest fixed-line network. Its leaders are members of the Communist Party first and businessmen second, similar to the Soviet system of the '80s. It owns circuits in China, Japan, Central America and South America, the Middle East, Australia, South Asia, Europe, and the United States. The government spun off China Mobile and China Satcom to help the growth into these markets. China Telecom still has the all the fixed land-lines under its control. Their undersea cables are in Hawaii and several places on the West Coast.[18] So, while they may seem like companies that just operate in China, they have arms with a long reach.

China Mobile is the largest mobile telephone operator in the world, having 70 percent of the domestic market. With so many people, they quickly get to a high number. They are 74 percent owned by the government, though as we saw after replacement of their CEO, 100 percent controlled by the Party.

China Unicom is the only state-owned telecom to be traded on the New York Stock Exchange, except that its two largest owners are both

Key Operating Data for China Mobile

	2011	2010
Customer Base (millions)	649.6	584
Net Additional Customers (millions)	65.6	61.7
3G Customer Base (millions)	51.2	20.7
Net Additional 3G Customers (millions)	30.5	15.2
Total Voice Usage (billions of minutes)	3,887.2	3,461.6
Average Revenue per User per Month (minutes per User, per month in RMB)	71	73
SMS Usage (billions of messages)	736.1	711
Wireless Data Traffic (billions of megabytes)	361.4	143.3

China Mobile has a global infrastructure to support its high number of users. This puts them deep into the infrastructure of the world's most powerful countries (China Mobile 2011 Annual Report, page 22).

state-owned, so it is a little difficult to think of them as "public" companies. It is the second largest telecom company after China Mobile. China Unicom and the Spanish telecom Telefonica are combining investments that they claim will be 10 percent of the world's market. Unicom gets a seat on Telefonica's board of directors. Through a separate deal, Telefonica and Vodaphone are sharing infrastructure in Europe, putting Huawei, which has separate deals with both of them, in a better position for expansion.

PCCW Limited, together with its subsidiaries, does telecommunications services primarily in Hong Kong, mainland China, the Middle East and the Asia Pacific regions. It offers local, mobile, and international telecommunications services, Internet access services, interactive multimedia and pay-TV services, computer, engineering, and other technical services. The company gets into investment and development of systems from offices in Hong Kong, mainland China, the Asia Pacific, and the Middle East. While U.S. and other foreign companies operate in China, they are not buying into its networks, but China is buying into everyone else's.

Because of the way international business has merged over the years, most of companies that own our communications systems are no longer just U.S. enterprises. We still have rules that limit the amount of ownership a foreign group can have, but limits do not mean "none." Just as simple examples, Vodafone from the U.K. and Verizon are teamed in Verizon Wireless; Vodafone owns part of a French telecom company that is being bought by Vivendi, a Paris based company; T-Mobile is a German wireless services provider, owned by Deutsche Telekom and soon to be bought by AT&T; the Alcatel-Lucent Technologies merger produced a company that does business in 130 countries and has employees with 100 nationalities. Acatel-Lucent, with its headquarters in Paris, is still ahead of Huawei in selling communications equipment. They include Bell Laboratories that did much of the original research that forms the underlying telecommunications infrastructure. Some of the large telecoms are government-owned or have substantial government control, so they are not much different from China.

The router that I use on Verizon is made in China and supplied by Vodaphone to my Verizon FIOS connection. As unhappy as I am about that, I am having trouble finding a router made in the U.S. The Chinese have the market locked up. A *Washington Post* article says NSA talked AT&T out of buying some equipment from them too; we already know about the Sprint/Nextel deal. I want to buy the router NSA buys. There is just too much going on in the world of business to keep up with it all, but it certainly is something that bears watching a little more closely. Routers are too important in directing Internet traffic to be left solely to the Chinese.

If they can't get to me directly, they can find another way. Vodaphone opened a joint research center in Italy with Huawei. Huawei just got a contract to replace 8000 wireless transmitters in Australia, on a Vodaphone contract. In a few years, all the 2G and 3G phones will be running on Huawei equipment, with a Huawei 3G phone to go with it. They got a 5-year deal to do managed services for Vodaphone's Ghana operations, and this relationship is just getting going. It is difficult to see exactly who you are buying from when the marketplace gets so complicated. The French company Vivendi is buying back its shares in French mobile carrier SFR from Vodaphone. That seems to look like a smart move. The French are careful about things that affect their national security.

Other governments and big businesses rent this infrastructure from the 58 major telecommunications companies, the same way an individual does — they buy service from them. What they don't do very often is control how these services are protected. So, among other things, I am happy with the way my Blackberry encrypts e-mail because I cannot rely on any of the vendors who sell me service to protect my e-mail in transit. They would say that was the customer's problem to deal with. From an infrastructure standpoint, the vendors would argue that they only lease circuits and the consumer of the service has to protect it from other people who might use the same service. This logic will not help those who do not have service if someone takes it away. I can use an example that makes practical sense to anyone, regardless of where you might work.

When I worked for the government, we had a contractor that was supposed to be designing a network that would be used to connect parts of a military command network, and it was going to put an infrastructure into place to start this work. The contractor wanted to lease the circuits from an undersea cable company that was owned by the Chinese and based in Hong Kong. From a security standpoint, it did not seem like a very good idea to have a cable that had actual connections to Mainland China and Hong Kong being used for such a critical function. Some might argue that if we can do banking this way, we surely can do anything else. We told the contractor this was not to be done and gave them the main reasons: the company was foreign owned; we did not trust the Chinese all that much; we didn't care that they were cheaper. This news did not even slow them down.

The next step was to bring in a Defense Security Service specialist in foreign ownership, control and influence. She explained the ownership of the company in question and how it was not wise to have a component of a command and control system riding on a network owned by another country, the Chinese aside. Having a Chinese owner made it impossible to consider such a move. They were not paying very much attention, or so it seemed, because they just kept plodding along towards that connection.

I went to see our general, who was a pretty sharp guy and saw what was happening. He said to bring it up at the staff meeting of our senior officers and he would take care of it. When it did, the general turned to the project manager with a look that would melt anyone who could look back, and said, "Is this true?" The contractor started to say that there were some very good reasons why we should consider buying these circuits, but he never got halfway through the argument when the director held up his hand. "Stop," he said. "I can't believe you were even considering doing this and I don't want to hear anymore about it." There was no argument from anyone and the meeting moved on to the next topic. They leased the service from a U.S. company.

I might have felt better if this was the only time a U.S. defense contractor ever put its business interests ahead of national security issues. We are going to regret not controlling this type of activity. If the Chinese escalate their Information War, things like this will matter. They will have control over our networks and can deny the use of them.

These services are like my FIOS connection to the Internet. If someone takes that from me, my data is still safe on my own computer, but I can't use the network to send e-mail or search for other data. In the case of war, I could have the military orders interrupted by having someone deny service to the network. A group of hackers that is mapping every computer in the United States is thinking about how to attack them all at once to deny sectors of the economy or military the use of those networks. We will still have our data but the infrastructure we need to use it will not be available. All the Chinese need to do is shut off those connections on every machine. And, they don't have to do it; they just have to demonstrate that they can. They can win, without firing a shot. Sun Tsu thought that was a good idea.

So, with all the communications equipment and circuits the Chinese have, they are close to being able to disrupt quite a bit of traffic in the world. They won't want anyone to see that, of course, but they are ready if the need arises. Before that happens, they will start trying to get people off of their protected networks and onto something they own or control. There are really two ways to do this kind of thing, besides the virus redirect I mentioned earlier.

The first is the "let me make you an offer you can't refuse" way. Make it cheap to buy into. They subsidize their vendors and teaming partners to make it cheaper to have their service than that of their competitors. They give low-interest loans and sweetheart deals to attract customers. They already proved they can do it with solar energy. It is really hard to say no to a good deal. They sell these services at the shop on the corner, using vendors we already know and use. They don't make a lot of money, but they do all right. If the companies are big enough, they can threaten smaller competitors to get with their companies. I haven't seen any instances where China has done this, but they certainly have the market power to do it.

The other way is to make the other services less attractive. If the Android operating system is free and can be used anywhere, try to make sure it works better on your phones than on anyone else's. Apps cannot work as well on other types of phones as on your own. Conversions of data cannot be as accurate and complete. Web interfaces cannot be as smooth. The idea is to intentionally influence that without getting caught. To do that, they have to be able to replace the operating system supplied by the original vendor. If they were the original vendor, it will be easy. If not, it can still be done, but it requires much more work.

If Blackberries are really secure, you might want to go after RIM and see if there was something to be done to make their products not work the way they should. They could make them look less attractive. That usually makes the other things on the market look better, even if they aren't. Earlier this year, when the Blackberries in Europe, then later in the U.S., started to have trouble with their equipment, I wondered how much of it came from China. A few of those routers they are faking can make a big difference in how a network will perform. Enough of them in the right places can cause a severe outage that is difficult to detect and impossible to correct without a long outage.

There are some software vendors (you might remember the browser battles a few years ago) that have been accused of this now and again. Users say their data didn't convert quite as well with one browser as with another. Imagine that. They called it "enhancing the user experience" in those days. One after another vendor was trying to say their browser was the best and the measure was how well it worked with other applications those vendors used. Some of them finally went bankrupt trying to keep up, and the market settled down a little. Driving out the competition is good for business.

Believing in War

There have not been very many wars where one country has opened up talks with, "We are going to pound you into dust and take all your territory. From then on, you will do things our way." Those are fighting words. It is never that simple. Usually the future combatants will start off by saying how great and wonderful everything is between them and how much they need each other. When enemies say that, there is trouble brewing. We aren't at that point with China just yet, but we will be.

Both Secretary of State Hillary Clinton and her deputy, Williams Burns, speak about U.S.–China relations as "challenging" and "sensitive." We could say that about Israel, France or Germany some days, so that doesn't tell us very much. They do say we are concerned about China's military build-up and their "incessant cyber attacks on public and private American entities." They are not happy about "bilateral economic priorities" which is State Department speak for trade imbalance, nor the Chinese ability to try to protect intellectual property of our businesses. And, of course, there is that little matter of the currency controls that are causing us no end of grief. They think we should talk more and they have set up some chances to do that with strategic security discussions. Considering the source of that, it is not much of a surprise that talking is always the best thing anyone can do for future relations. More talk (frank discussions) means more trust, the way the State Department looks at things. State always wants to talk, and the Defense Department wants to send ships. Neither of those will work very well.

The Chinese would be the first to say they are just commercial people, trading with the rest of the world. They are doing things that every other country does and doing it better than the rest. They are not at war with anyone. There are plenty of Henry Kissingers of the world who really want to believe them, but those State Department folks are saying we should talk and they are saying it with the background of some clashes that are starting to concern them.

Most rational people do not want to be at war with anyone, but they also know the difference between war and *not war*. Sometimes it is just a matter of intent. Aleksandr Solzhenitsyn, the Russian writer, said: "If only there were evil people somewhere, insidiously committing evil deeds, and it were necessary only to separate them from the rest of us and destroy them. But the line dividing good and evil cuts through the heart of every human being." It isn't about whether they are nice people or not. It has to be measured by what they do. They look like the devil to me.

The Chinese really believe they are the world's strongest nation, without having the most powerful military. They haven't been growing their military steadily, but it was not a priority for them. They have been growing their businesses, especially those that related to networks of all kinds, because they believe control of information will help to equalize things between countries stronger than they are. How many countries are stronger than they are? Just one.

They have a centralized management that can direct how they build themselves, but they have a long way to go to become the type of world power that we are. They buy up the world's communications systems and put deep roots into them. They hack everyone and they steal business secrets from everybody, not just us. They have the ability to control their Internet but that hacking continues like it is part of the accepted practice of the government that owns the capability. They are trying to get their state-owned companies into every network the world has. They back off when discovered, and try again a different way. They spy, like everyone else, just more often. Over time, they have gravitated to this kind of war because it is more successful and less dangerous than the alternatives. They like it this way, because they are winning, and they are glad to talk, stall and delay in any way they can.

If you go back and read the definition of Information War, the way RAND laid it out for us, they are doing everything by the book. They may have changed it a little to fit their culture and way of communicating to their Army, but it is pretty close. It looks and feels like war.

Deterrence

It would be nice if they couldn't get away with this sort of thing, but we can't just say, "Stop" and expect them to pay attention. We have to make it more difficult to continue. Since they are not going to help us out by telling us what to do, it is not as easy as we would hope.

Talking might help with the economic warfare, because the European Union and the U.S. are not the only entities in the world that are behind in their loan payments to China. There is enough resentment to get something going to put pressure on them. That is the kind of thing State and Commerce Departments can do. But they can't do much about Chinese intentions in the cyber war and space, as in outer space. These are things that need deterrence to slow them down.

Deterrence is a kind of threat that something bad will happen if the behavior isn't changed. If my dog nips my hand, I smack him with a newspaper. If it happens a few times, I don't have to smack him; I just pick up the newspaper and start looking at dog ads. He behaves without having to be hit. So far, the Chinese can thumb their noses at anything we can say we will do to them if they don't stop. We don't have a good deterrent strategy for China.

They are like a big bully who is at the bus stop where our neighbor sends her children. She can drive the children to the bus stop and wait with them until the bus comes, or she can call this boy's parents and talk to them about his behavior. She can call the police if some violence is done. She can call the school because in this part of Virginia, children can be disciplined in school for what they do waiting for the bus or getting off the bus and going home. She can train her child to fight. She can hire a guard. These are all things she could do, but sitting in the car at the bus stop works, so she hasn't looked for another alternative. She has a deterrent. The bully knows she can get out of the car and stop his behavior because she is bigger than he is and has some status. He would look bad hitting a woman, so he can't really do very much.

Deterring a country is harder than stopping a bully, but some of the same principles apply. The most important is the threat has to be credible. I wanted to go over to the bus stop and threaten the little brat with bodily harm, but that is not a credible threat. It might be a crime, and I'm sure the little guy can read, and knows it. Those mothers sitting in their cars would not let that happen, either. One of them might be his mother, but I doubt it. It wouldn't matter. They will defend any of those kids, even the bad ones.

Our leaders seem to think that talking about this will turn the Chinese around, but that is not going to help. We have to pay attention to them. The White House might remember Norm Augustine, the CIO of Martin Marrietta, when it merged with Lockheed. He said it was not so important for an executive to do something; they just have to pay attention to it and the right kinds of things will usually happen. We need to start paying attention to what they are doing and what can be done to stop them.

Having someone else have a chokehold on the world's telecommunications is not what we thought about 20 years ago when the military was planning for Information War. We owned the Internet then, and many people outside the U.S. still think we do now. Not true. The shoe is on the other foot and it hurts, but it doesn't hurt enough. We have to have more interest to stop the kind of things the Chinese are trying to do, and we have to believe it is war.

We thought we could get their attention with some trade sanctions and some letters to the WTO, but that didn't work very well. They need a dose of their own medicine, by having our government share limited amounts of intelligence with businesses trading with China. We have a really good intelligence community and we don't use it very much for the kind of things that will help us here. We have executive orders that prevent it, but we need to think about changing some of those.

It is not like it is a secret that the dictators of the world are squirreling money away. Look at what happened when Gaddafi and Mubarak were missing in action. Their money was being "assessed" by every major bank in the world. After the Middle East settled down everyone started following the money trail. The new countries wanted it, other governments wanted it; banks wanted it too. We have made it illegal to give these leaders money, and the rest of the world probably thinks that is funny.

I would like to know who is producing counterfeit goods and where they are being sold. I can't stop China from selling them internally, but I can stop them from being sold outside the country, if we start focusing on it and giving resources to people who do that sort of thing. Let's spend some money trying to discover or stop it. The Chinese can have all of those counterfeits they want. They fall apart in a few months, so they deserve them.

Our intelligence community has a great amount of talent for reverse engineering things. It would be nice if they could apply some of that to identifying stolen trade secrets being incorporated in Chinese goods. It would be nice if they could find some fake systems or some of that software going into our infrastructure. We would have some real information to give the WTO then, and it can be used to sue U.S. subsidiaries of some of those companies.

Our national business leaders naively believe that we can "out-innovate" China by just doing what we have always done, but checking the number of new research facilities in China and China's teaming with various researchers outside the country, that is not very realistic. We are selling them the ability to compete with us now, and in the future.

I want to know more about those PLA businesses operating in the United States. It needs to be harder for them to operate here. Much harder. We can do what they did to Google and shut off their power every now and again. We have lots of trouble with power anyway. I don't like the idea of them being allowed to operate here. I want to make sure I don't buy a washer from one of them.

But, the worst problem we have, and the one that is most difficult, is hacking. We could try stopping their hacking by jamming their sites, using logic bombs and Trojan horses or any number of other things to disrupt their hacking networks. It seems like this should work, but it never does, because the hackers use legitimate sites to store their attack software and data they have retrieved. They are not hacking us directly. We might be attacking some furniture company in Iowa or a clothing store in my own town. When we find them, they just move to another place. Hackers understand deterrence as well as anyone, and they like to avoid it.

Every president in the last 25 years has said we need better trained people to handle computer security, when what we need is less security and more deterrence. Nobody in the government has figured out how to do that yet.

We can broaden our diplomatic effort to see if we can appeal to the federal government to talk to the Chinese directly. Before you laugh at this, it works once in awhile with criminal gangs stealing money or information from more than one company, though China is not a country that cooperates very much. I was occasionally surprised by how much cooperation there can be between countries on criminal matters. Our law enforcement has even gotten some help from the Russian government and most of our allies, but it does not seem to work with China, Iran or Slovakia. There could be a few reasons for this, but not any that would favor China, Iran or Slovakia's image.

We can spend a lot more money on security of our systems and try to keep people out by making our target harder to get to. This is the equivalent of having a guard sitting with the children at the bus stop, only it doesn't work nearly as well. It used to be the way of business people everywhere, using the philosophy that you don't have to run faster than the bear, you just have to run faster than the person with you on the trail. That doesn't work anymore. Now that they can attack everyone at once; nobody is very safe. It makes the board of a corporation feel better, but it has very little deterrent value. The hackers know they can get in.

We are running out of options here, for a reason. There is almost nothing that deters this type of activity, especially where the government cooperates in protecting the people doing it. For trade, spying and hacking, the rules for deterrence are basically the same. If we are nice, there is no deterrent.

We tried to play nice in trade and it got our trade deficit raised every day by Chinese currency manipulation. In hacker circles, we publish the list of Internet addresses where these people operate from and they move their operations. We block them and they try a new method of attack. We can neuter them sometimes by modifying their software but that only works for a while and a new version is out that works. Most businesses are too slow for that to work.

The real problem is there are ways to deter trading schemes we have seen the Chinese use, and we can deal with hackers by making their lives more difficult and painful, but it requires our government to target them and undermine them. They are not willing to do that. Too many lawyers tell them they shouldn't. We need some new lawyers.

In the case of this type of hacking, I have to agree with that Chinese General who said the only way we can deter such a thing is to have those capabilities ourselves ... and more of them. We need to increase our attack forces and turn them loose. Find out what our enemy is doing and how they are doing it. Bury ourselves deep inside those operations and head off their plans before they can get us surrounded. The world saw how hard it was to deal with a group like Anonymous, which is not very big and is not backed by a government. This is a much bigger operation and has been going on longer. We can stop building fighter planes and tanks for a few months and start building up our computer forces.

We should help industry too, but not the way we do it now. The Defense Department seems to be able to help defense contractors by giving them classified information about the attacks against their computer systems. They need to start giving it to anyone who is being attacked. Defense used to classify the sources of attacks that were occurring in industry and then only give the summaries out to companies with clearances. Oftentimes, they were denying that information to the companies that reported it to begin with. It made no sense then, nor does it now. We spend too much money on collecting the information about who is hacking us, then never giving it to the people who need it.

We don't have the stomach for Information War. We have to go after the people on the other side of this with a vengeance. Attack them. Disrupt them. Infect them. As long as we don't, they win. If we don't stop them now, we have a bigger war to engage in. it will be much easier to fight them now, then wait for their successes to make it more difficult in the future. They are not unwilling to use real war if they think they will win.

Almost Real War

What Von Clausewitz reminded everyone of was that wars should be fought without regard to how bad it might be. The Chinese and Russians seem to be considering war in a way that crosses a line between information war and nuclear war. That is not a fine line to most of us.

The person who invented information warfare in China wrote a book called *World War: The Third World War—Total Information War*. This is a long title for a book, but the Chinese characters make it look shorter. His thoughts he expressed are shorter too. He was concerned that China is vulnerable to information war in a slightly different form. He talks about those with the weapons of war, whether computers or nuclear weapons and how they have first strike and second strike capability. It always amazes me how military people can talk about mass destruction of millions of people like it was an X-Box first-person shooter.

The Russians and Americans always talked about this in the context of nuclear weapons and who would use them first. Both of them said they never would, but they both had them. Since the Chinese do too, we already know that game pretty well. They say they will not use them first, but they are undecided about when a first strike might be necessary. We say that we will not use them first, but we keep submarines out in the ocean with them, just in case. The Chinese have nuclear submarines with missiles on them too, so that part balances out pretty well. Numbers are not so important when the weapons are nuclear. A few can go a long way towards deterring one another. If the Chinese want to deter someone from launching a first strike, they have to have the weapons to launch a second strike. This is called first strike deterrence because it keeps the other side from thinking about launching one.

Now, this is not as simple as it sounds because the Chinese view of what might be a first strike might not be the kind of war we are thinking about. If we go back to that Chinese general who said he thought we might just throw up a nuclear weapon if the U.S. decides to break out weapons in defense of Taiwan, he was not talking about dropping one on Los Angeles the way we dropped one on Nagsaki; he was talking about shooting it off in the air, high up. There is no nuclear blast incinerating houses like we saw in those training films made in the1950s, or a large fireball sprouting up out of the ground. There is just a flash and nothing. Well, "nothing" may not be the right term, since it is really nothing anyone can see. It is something called an electromagnetic pulse (EMP) and it is not very nice.

EMP can do in one minute what nuclear bombs can do, but they don't leave such a mess. They don't kill very many people, but they are hard on power lines, automobiles and telecommunications circuits. Nothing that has a circuit will work unless those circuits are hardened against EMP. We can think of being without electricity for a while, but it would not be fun to be without electricity, cell phones, cars, trucks, portable computers, circuit breakers, back-up generators, water purification, ATMs, banks, and most battery operated emergency devices. In a published report a few years ago, a congressional panel thought these effects might be a circle around 700 miles.[19] That would be a long way to walk to the grocery store, which will be empty by the time we get there.

The only good thing about this type of attack is the deterrence value of having the same type of weapon in your own inventory. That would certainly make China, Iran and Russia think twice before letting one of these go, but North Korea will be on that list next year and they don't seem quite as stable or dependent on the same types of technology that the rest of us are. A country like North Korea might get along fine without electricity or any of those other things. They may not have them now.

Nuclear weapons are usually a sure sign of war. When someone starts setting one off, whether it is high up or not, it is going to cause some real problems because the next step is for us to do the same thing back to them. If North Korea sets it off, then we are tempted to do the same to them. The Chinese would say it is a shame that they can't control North Korea, but they are our friends in a strange sort of way, and we will protect them if they are attacked. It is a tricky situation, but the people in Los Angeles want something to happen and they are tired of eating food out of a can. We hit those North Koreans with something they can remember for a year or so, then we have to deal with China.

Once that starts, it can be difficult to control. That first explosion detonates over Pyongyang, and then what? Do we both just sit and wait to see how that worked out for us? Remember that his comments were related to Taiwan, so in the meantime, the Chinese are overrunning Taiwan, which is not very big and would not long for that to be over. We might not even see China as the opening round of this war. None of the options are very good, particularly for us, and even China probably does not like the scenarios they have put together for this type of event. Radiation is not very pleasant for any of us.

They want Taiwan back and think it was given to them after World War II. They think we are responsible for it not being given back. They just would not want to start throwing nuclear weapons to get it. But, the Chinese general mentioned another type of thing besides nuclear weapons — viruses.

Viruses don't make a mess either, and they are not usually seen as war. They don't produce radiation or burn up children. They are clean, so to speak. We have even managed to get a virus in our Predator drone systems and I can't imagine the kind of idiocy that has allowed that to happen. You would think, with the importance of this weapon to killing off terrorists and doing surveillance of the ground in Afghanistan, that our military would be a little more careful with it. What are they thinking? They are lucky to still have a drone system to work with.

These are not the kind of viruses done by kids who are using a virus kit that they got off the Internet. Those are known viruses and the anti-virus companies spend quite a bit of time keeping track of the development of them. The type the general is talking about are combat viruses, and these will not be floating around on the Internet waiting for someone to figure out how they work. These are viruses that are intended to be damaging to a specific part of the infrastructure like the Stuxnet worm was to Iran's centrifuges. There was speculation that they worm was spread by an Israeli agent that intentionally entered it into the systems using a portable memory stick.[20] This helps them be a little more controllable, but nobody knows how controllable they will be. We do know they are good sight better than a nuke.

Symantec did an analysis, by country, on where the Stuxnet worm showed up. (Just as an aside, after CIFUS overruled a takeover of Symantec, the anti-virus company, it formed Huawei Symantec Technologies Co. Ltd. Huawei is the majority partner with 51 percent ownership, with the business headquarters in Chengdu, China. In November 2011, Huawei announced it was buying the rest of the company from Symantec.)

Though not in large numbers, the worm got into systems in India and Indonesia, more often than it did in Iran. Since these are reported incidents, the Iran number could be a little short of reality, but we will never know. Pakistan, Indonesia, Afghanistan, United States, and Malaysia were all places where it weaseled itself in. Now, it appears that this particular worm would only attack the control software for certain types of equipment, but the software was used in more applications than just centrifuges. It is more difficult to control things like this than to talk about them, because the unintended consequences are not nearly as easy to see in a laboratory where they are built. Second, the effects are not nearly as predictable as the developers think they will be. Software developers think their software is always perfect, even if the Internet is not. Things will happen that they did not anticipate. They will say "Oops, sorry," but the driver of the car that crashes into the train is saying a good bit more.

So, suppose we have a virus that brings down the electric grid, or a good part of it. Doomsday, you might think. This will cause quite a bit of intentional damage that will cause us to start thinking our national security is at stake. We tend to roll our nuclear subs and airplanes at times like that, so it isn't something someone is going to do without a lot of thought.

Our government will want to hunt for the country that did this. There will be some unintentional damage (sometimes called collateral damage) to clean up because more things are on the electronic grid than war planners tend to think about. We saw this when hurricanes brought down power lines to large patches of land. That fellow across the street cannot live much longer than the 4-hour battery life on his dialysis machine. My mom says the food will last a few days in the refrigerator after a Florida hurricane. Hospitals have quite a few people who require constant care and many of them will eventually run out of power. Knocking out the electric grid will put everyone in the dark, with no street lights or traffic signals, making emergency calls more interesting. If we don't have TV, there will certainly be a revolution.

The police forces are pretty busy, but crime goes to nothing. There is a good trade-off there. We won't be eating out as often, but crime will be down. I can live with that.

Emergency generators will work for those who have them. The rest of us will not be eating quite so well, *and* not eating out. I will get testy after a week of eating out of a can, so I may lead the revolution. Guns may come out, and we may need some police in my neighborhood.

Getting fuel for generators and cars is a little more complicated, but it may be possible. There is a manual pump that is available for emergencies that would allow people to pump fuel out like old-fashioned well water. Most cities have backup power for sewer and water, but rural areas may rely on batteries that won't last forever.

The real problem is that the electrical grids are not all in the U.S. and they are interconnected, so someone who tries a virus will find it in places it should not really be, even in some allied government's grid. The Canadians, Brazilians, Central Americans and Mexicans will not like having that virus in their systems. It could get into international grids and turn out to be harder to control than those folks who worked in the lab thought it was. Oops. This would be annoying to the leadership. Global war is complicated, and just as complicated and risky for the Chinese as us.

Eventually, we are going to figure out that it was a virus and start working on a solution that will reduce its damage or get rid of it. This might take a few weeks, or less, if we are lucky. Some portions of the grid might not be affected. Maybe we can figure out why that is and fix it for all the places. These types of things do not last forever, so using them is not something a person would do without quite a bit of thought. Figuring out who did it will be possible, but it may take months. It can ultimately be traced back to its country of origin, maybe to a place. Then, we have to figure out what to do about it. That is the hard part.

The nice thing about lining up armies to fight is, we usually don't have to wait to figure out who it was that we fought. With viruses, that takes time. At Pearl Harbor, it was pretty easy to see the meatballs on the side of the airplanes coming into drop bombs on our ships and people. This would not be like that. I think people are confused when they say there could be a digital Pearl Harbor. It won't be that simple.

After we answer the question of who did it, the next obvious question anyone in this situation has to answer is, "Is it war?" This will be important to all those soldiers and sailors on nuclear submarines that are moving toward South East Asia by now. Some people have published reports that the Chinese and Russians have already gotten into our electric grid and planted software that makes it easier to come back and do more, potentially to disrupt operations on the grid. There was even some speculation that the Chinese had something to do with some widespread outages in the grid, happening last year.[21] These articles don't strike me as very credible, but it doesn't answer the question.

If both of those things were true — the Russians and Chinese got into our electric grid and planted software to get back into it and disrupt it, and they had actually done it, to prove that they could — would that be an act of war? Probably not. We would like to think it was, but it is like the gunman who holds up a person on the street with a finger in his jacket pocket. You couldn't charge him with armed robbery with a finger. If we believe he has a gun, we might defend ourselves, right then, as if he had a gun. They run that risk. They would rely on us knowing they planted the software, but didn't do anything that would cause us harm. We have to know that they are doing this for some reason that looks like war, and that is as close as it gets to war, without pushing things over the line. That is just how the Chinese work, pushing us right up to the limit to see what happens.

First, for those who say the Russians and Chinese did this, we have the little problem of attribution, again. The software might have some programming that we can recognize from somewhere in China, but that won't prove much. Can I say that because the attack took place from a city in China that the government of China actually was doing it? If a criminal gang did it for extortion, do we blame China for it? If North Korea did it, would we blame China? Then, what do we tell our guys in those nuclear subs? "Wait, while we figure this out."

You can go to war with a group of people in another country, as we have done with al-Qaeda, but they usually have to do something to you that justifies that. China would not like us fighting with people inside its borders, even if they were doing some terrible things. It is a much harder problem than just declaring that someone is doing something bad and needs to get whacked for it. So, do we have to wait around for them to do something really bad to act? Only if we want to go to war. As you remember, nobody goes to war these days, so let's not.

Terrorism

The White House accurately said that the main risk we face right now is the migration of cyberwar techniques to terrorists.[22] Their point is that governments have been in control of real cyberwar, while the rest of us are looking at thieves and extortionists on the fringe. This is good deception on all fronts. Terrorism is not war most of the time, but it looks a lot like it. It is more of a substitute for war because the people involved do not usually have the ability to wage war on anyone. They may not be a country or have any permanent place to live. This gives attribution a whole new meaning.

China has been willing to allow terrorists to harbor themselves in some of their best friends' borders, Iran and Pakistan being right up there with the best of them. Since most of China's neighbors and friends become the source of the trouble in the world, we can probably figure out that they are not going to see this much differently.

Syria, which seems to be best friends with Russia and China, has said there are a number of terrorists in their country that are causing disruptions. To show how happy they were about anyone in Europe trying to do what they did in Libya, they released some of those terrorists that they have held for us since the 9/11 attacks. How closely they held them might be a question, but they weren't causing any problems we could see.

Syria says the real terrorists are arming themselves and trying to overthrow the government. In order to crack down on them, they are lobbing mortars, which are not the most accurate of things, into the city of Hom. Counterterrorism experts all over the world are wondering what the connection is between mortars and terrorists, since it is Syria that looks like terrorists and not the other way around. So, we can't always believe that terrorists are what we think they are, especially if we are getting our information from governments that clearly are not our friends.

There are gradients of terrorism. We have a group like Sum Shinrikyo that tried to gas people in Japan with sarin nerve gas, or the Symbianese Liberation Army (not to be confused with the Nokia operating system of the same name) which was going around California robbing banks to finance their growth, and claiming to be a group that would change the world. It turned out that change would come by killing a school superintendant and kidnapping Patty Hearst from her apartment. There about 150 or so of these groups like the PLO, Al Queda, the Shining Path and the Red Brigade that are up to various kinds of trouble that only rarely reaches us in North America. That could change.

Anonymous is something we know about but it is not what I call a terrorist group, even though there are many who say it is. I'm not sure

Anonymous is really trying to cause harm, as much as they are exposing the general state of security on the Internet. But you can imagine a group with the same type of skill that was intent on causing harm to the U.S. government or the military. When a ship fired cruise missiles at Osama Bin Laden, the Navy had the names and quite a bit of personal information on the ship's crew posted on the Internet. In retrospect, it was not a clever thing to do, but nothing came of it. A terror group that was intent on making trouble can be waiting for this type of thing to happen again. The Internet is used for far too many things that are not good for our safety, but the governments of the world are addicted to the Internet and don't know how to quit using it.

I don't like to think about the possibilities if Iran is encouraged to try out some of the same types of terrorist tools used in Stuxnet, or if they encourage other people to shift their emphasis away from blowing up people. It is one thing for China to do it, since we will ultimately find out they did and it could lead to war. If Iran does it, much the same as North Korea firing a missile or doing a nuclear test, China will say, "Oh, those bad boys are stirring up trouble again!" It is war by proxy that we have seen from them before.

When it comes to terrorism against information, there hasn't been much to be seen. A *New York Times* article, after the World Trade Center was bombed the first time, said the secondary target for that attack was the telephone switching center in Lower Manhattan. If that is true, somebody was thinking about what a disruption that kind of attack would make and may have ruled it out. It doesn't kill very many people, but it sure does do a lot of damage to commerce. They were already thinking along those lines before they decided on disrupting it with airplanes. Terrorists like to kill a lot of people and computers are not really very good at that, as much as some movie makers would like to have us believe the opposite.

A national magazine asked me to list the type of attacks that I thought terrorists might make against our infrastructure. I didn't want to do it because I believe they are working on such things right now but may not have thought of all of the possibilities. There is no point in encouraging them to do better. Some of our freelance writers and a few national authors have come up with better ideas than the Chinese or any terrorist group might invent on their own. I wish these writers spent more time on what we might do to deter them.

There is evidence to suggest the Russians and Chinese are planning to develop a capability to shut down the electrical grid, and may have tested it already, but that can be a hedge against war and not necessarily a show of their intentions. Governments do this all the time to show each other that they can make trouble if we don't all get along and let them have their way. All countries have these types of capabilities to make war that are never discussed in public and may never be used anywhere. If terrorists shut down the electric grid, and they do it from electronic bases in China, we have the worst of situations. Who do we retaliate against, and how are the Chinese going to take it?

In the 9/11 terrorist attacks, the hijackers were mostly from Saudi Arabia. We certainly didn't launch attacks against that country for what its citizens did and it was clear, in that case, where they came from. We went after a group that was well hidden and did pretty well at getting rid of some of them. If they were hiding in Iran it might be more difficult. If they were hiding in China, or were given electronic connections through them, it would be harder still. We already know that RBS went to China, so maybe there are more of these folks that are doing a migration there.

Attribution will not be so simple in an electronic attack. Probably for that reason alone, the best capability a government can have is the ability to reach into the world's networks and know who is responsible for what types of activity. We have to be able to do this better than any other country if we are going to have both warning and response capabilities. That is spying, even though it might be for defensive purposes. We can't talk about it, but we do have to do it. We have to be deep into the electronic networks of countries who don't want us there, looking at groups who really don't want us doing that. There is no other way to defend against this type of attack, either by preventing it or attacking the real source of it.

The fact that other countries will not like us doing this will make it more difficult. We may have a few civil libertarians say it is illegal to do this sort of thing, but most of them know better. Neither of these should deter us.

7

The New Cold War

We have always believed that ordnance on target wins wars, so we have some really big weapons like aircraft carriers, as big as a city of 5000. We build lots of expensive airplanes that can carry bombs or shoot down other airplanes and we think those will help us some day. We have some experienced fighters after Iraq and Afghanistan and whole shiploads of Strikers and personnel carriers. If we haven't given them away, they might be useful for the wars we learned to fight.

We know where to put a bomb (Actually, there was that one time in Belgrade, when we bombed the Chinese embassy by accident) or how to get it there in one piece and make sure it doesn't kill a whole house full of innocent people, and the idea of the bomb is important to winning wars. One of those al–Qaeda in Iraq or Taliban leaders can understand a bomb on the front of a missile, strapped to the wing of a Predator or Reaper, as easily as we understood the plane striking the World Trade Center. We see ourselves at war with al–Qaeda, but it is harder to see that we are at war with China. We don't want the same kind of war with both of them, so we think we cannot be at war with China.

If you saw the fight that broke out when Georgetown's basketball team went to China to play a Chinese Army team, you saw just a brief glimpse of the feelings involved. It is easy to dismiss it as the heat of the moment in a sporting event, but the look on the faces of those Army team members as they were kicking and hitting the Georgetown player on the floor gave me the feeling that there was more to it than just a basketball game. There was real hate there. They were frustrated and they were not going to take it anymore. Somebody in that Army, maybe above the Army, was steering them in that direction.

We have to believe that too much power has been placed in the government in China. The military influences how their economy expands and how the civilian structure is used. They grow by doing business that is not altogether what the plan says it should be. There were indications in the case of the Queensway Group that the Chinese senior leaders were trying to put distance between themselves and some of the companies' activities. They found it hard to do. Even the planners know they are a little out of control. This is dangerous.

China's military is not friendly to the U.S., and "not friendly" is not really descriptive enough of the feelings. The secretary of defense said the display of the J-20 fighter was not something President Hu Jintau seemed to have been aware of, meaning the military thought it was useful to use the secretary's visit as a show of force, and may have acted alone in doing it. There are also divisions between the army and police, who run the border patrol functions,[1] which has the sea lanes and fishing rights being enforced by non-military forces. They are in a constant struggle for influence between and among themselves and the Central Committee. They can criticize military exercises of the U.S. in front of the chairman of the Joint Chiefs, who was on an official visit to China. It makes diplomatic relations more difficult and it shows that the military might not be as constrained by political oversight as we would want. We certainly are, so we think they are too. Every time there is confrontation with the West, the military is stronger. We need to tamp this down and do it in a way that is politically acceptable to both civilian governments.

Probably the best alternative is another Cold War. I am not a politician and this is not a political solution, but we already have a Cold War, so we might as well recognize it. We are not at war with anyone, and we don't call it war. We don't have to call it Cold War either, but I can't think of another name. We need to learn to fight the Information War, on the scale that they are doing it. That is more difficult.

Borders

Every country has a physical border. Over the years those borders have been surveyed and staked out with signs and security that check for various types of banned substances and make sure everyone who comes in is allowed to be here. We believe this is part of our national security. We seem to have quite a bit of difficulty with defending that boundary, but we have not had quite so much trouble defining it. One historian I know says survey crews were sent out for the express purpose of defining our national boundaries so we knew what was ours. It has changed over time, thorough wars and negotiations (we gave some land back to Mexico during the Kennedy administration), but we recognize the importance of a border. In networks, we don't.

I went to Vermont once and said, "How is it possible to defend such a territory from anyone coming across when there are no roads in some places and trees growing up everywhere?" "It isn't," said a farmer who was selling vegetables along the road, "We keep an eye out for strangers."

At one level we have the most elaborate of airport screening, border crossing points with INS and customs officials checking bags, X-ray machines for cargo vessels, a system for visas and passports, and all of the rest that goes with it. But, we also have a bunch of farmers in northern Vermont who keep a look out for strangers passing through. They have to because we could not protect everything to the same level we protect airports and main border crossings. We just can't protect everything.

We have no such concept for our network infrastructure. As a practical matter, jurisdiction in information systems has always been defined by ownership and demarcation points.[2] The IT community has adopted this idea. The demarc is where my ownership responsibility ends. Because ownership is the key, national boundaries are not usually considered. Of course, this makes it more interesting.

So, how do I know when information I am sending crosses over into Canada? I don't, and it does sometimes. Most people would say, I don't care. But I think we do want to know, and we do care. Defining these boundaries does three things. First, it establishes dominion, i.e. who owns it. Second, it defines responsibility — what legal entity is responsible for the network? Third, it establishes legal authority. We probably cannot protect every network in the U.S. even if we wanted to, but we could come closer to identifying and defending the most important ones if we knew where they were, what laws they were bound by and who owned them. Then, we can teach people to look for strangers in places we can't get to.

If we were to define the national networks in the same way, we would find that they are not all in the U.S., and they do not pay much attention to the physical borders of other countries. Every now and again, when I send my e-mail through my Blackberry, I am reminded that the mail goes to Canada first and then to the delivery point. I am OK with that, but it is an example of the problem with national boundaries and electronic boundaries. There is no border crossing involved in what I send to Canada and nobody (that I know of) looks at the e-mails I send. We have good relations with Canada and we have investigated many computer crimes with them, so I don't think much about it. But the same thing does not apply to Russia, Iran, Syria and China. I'm not quite as happy with people from other countries who might offer hosted services for me to use, or visit us without going through any kind of checkpoint or identifying themselves. It is certainly time to start thinking about this, but is going to take a very long time to actually do much about it. We don't have that much time.

Hurry Up and Run

The first step in this is to recognize that this is war, and the Chinese favor it not being a shooting war. This is a good thing for us, but may not last forever. The capabilities of fighting an Information War are not in our military. It should be, because that is where the doctrine came from, but the military is not capable of fighting it. They can't fight in the civilian infrastructure where most of it is being carried out now. The White House is dealing with a very simple problem in consideration of a House bill that will allow exchanges of information between the government and commercial industry. We had this same argument when I was there. The Republicans are mouthing the words of the software and hardware vendors who would not like to be held responsible for security of their products. The Democrats are mouthing the words of a few national security agencies that think they can "help" the commercial sector do a better job. That might even be true, but we don't want it that much.

The companies that operate the national infrastructure for us have to do it, and somebody is going to have to pay them to do it. The disadvantage of an open system like ours is not everyone does things because it is the right thing to do. This one very small issue is driven by congressional paralysis. It does not even reach the point of discussion in most talk about protecting the national infrastructure from potential attacks.

We have difficulties with having someone in charge when it comes to protecting the critical networks of the U.S. They don't belong to any one place, and the government tries to manage it without having the authority needed to do it. In China, even in some of the democracies of the world, the government owns everything and has centralized authority over the companies that operate it. We have no such structure, and there is not much sentiment anywhere for having the same thing here. The only problem is that voluntary protection of the critical systems cannot be done. There are really only three choices: (1) nationalize the businesses that maintain critical infrastructures; (2) develop financial incentives for commercial businesses to keep it safe from our enemies, and keep China from buying their way in; (3) let the military do it for us.

I don't like the idea of nationalizing anything, but some people do. Most countries actually do. Our enemies would never think of allowing anyone other than a government to control the telecommunications or electrical infrastructure. They own it, operate it, and control it. So, they start with an advantage in war with anyone because they have the control they need.

We could try to incentivize the civilian owners of the infrastructure. This sounds strange to some people, but the ownership of telecoms and services is a private matter. We could wave a flag and tell all of the owners to increase their security and build up their defenses. In fact, we have done that a few times and the business people I worked with did try to do better at protecting their resources, but they have a market share to maintain and profitability is more important to shareholders than national security. The government always loses out in the end. The only way to make it work for them is to create financial incentives to maintain a level of security that is "best practice for the industry." There is quite a bit of disagreement about what that is, but there are working groups and standards agencies that can figure it out. What is does mean, though, is paying for any improvements that might be required, and that is more difficult — actually the main reason we have not done it. The alternative is to let someone do the protection that is already being paid by the government.

When Cyber Command, a new military defense command, was being formed in 2009, there was an attempt to have all of Homeland Security's infrastructure protection efforts under what was then part of the National Security Agency. So, not only were we talking about putting it under military control, but under the spy agency that is responsible for monitoring signals intelligence all over the world. Lots of people thought this was a really bad idea, and I was one of them.

Congress held up the establishment of Cyber Command for several months because of the issue. The Defense Department had to issue a formal memo saying that Cyber Command's authority would only extend to dot mil (.mil) addresses, i.e. those which are owned and operated by the military services and agencies. That doesn't include utilities, the Internet, or private businesses. It was no secret why Congress was so against having the military involved in what is a decidedly a business owned and operated by commercial businesses. They have no authority there.

What happened in 1986 was a decision that most people see as innocuous — making the National Institute of Standards and Technology (NIST) responsible for standards to protect unclassified information in computer systems. Congress decided that the National Security Agency had a lane, and it wanted that lane to be in national security, fitting as that might seem. Senator John McCain from Arizona, in an argument at the time, might have had us believe that critical infrastructure is part of the national assets that might be "helped" by participation of the military arm of national security, when that was never intended and should be stamped out before it gains any more life. It seems he may have forgotten what the debate over the Computer Security Act was all about.

The act was passed for many reasons, but just one example is the meddling in commercial affairs of a small company that sold engineering information over commercial networks. The Defense Department decided to "intervene" by sending a representative out to this company and advising them that some of the information they were selling would give an advantage to Russia where some of it was being sold. The company did not take this well, explaining that it was commercial engineering knowledge that was not designated as national defense information, and they could basically sell it to anyone who could afford it. They then called every congressman in their district to complain. Congress was listening.

The Computer Security Act gave responsibility for policy making to the National Institute of Standards and Technology, for unclassified, and NSA for classified information. That was the surface decision, but it was clear on Capitol Hill that nobody wanted the NSA involved in the commercial side of protection, and they still don't. In a succession of acts since, there has been a clear dividing line between the military, NSA, law enforcement and the civil sector. Homeland Security, which came along later, took over many of these responsibilities. They are often criticized, for all the right reasons, because they are not competent at leading the kind of efforts needed to secure our country's most important assets. The people who usually do this critique are in the military and intelligence communities who really believe they could do better. There is no doubt of the truth of that.

It reminds me of the times when we were debating the new subject of computer crime and Willis Ware at RAND said it was possible to stop computer crime by doing something very simple — putting an informant in every data center. Only he added, in that case, we would have to think long and hard about the cost of the solution. He was right about it at that time, and it is no different today. The cost of having the military involved in our civilian infrastructure comes at a very high price. They have a role, to be sure, but that role is not the leadership of the civilian communities that make up our infrastructure. That should really belong to our telecommunications businesses.

It would mean defining the infrastructure much more narrowly than we do now. In an effort to be all-inclusive, we have long list of businesses that "own" the National Infrastructure. We cannot have the banking communities, rail and airline transport, software companies, and computer companies deciding how the infrastructure should be protected and getting resources to do it. This dilutes the issue and makes it harder to focus resources, which are difficult enough to get. We need to concentrate on the telecommunications companies that actually carry everyone else and directly fund them. Government has been notoriously bad at spending the billions of dollars already being allocated, and I can give two examples of it to show the point.

In 1996, the Ballistic Missile Defense Organization (BMDO) funded a substantial amount of the information technology budgets of Redstone Arsenal, in Huntsville, Alabama, which had the major military components of Army that built and maintained missile systems needed for command and control, business systems, and design capabilities for contractors. We had advised them the year before that we wanted to do a regional assessment of security of their networks, looking at contractor and government systems as if they were one network, so they were especially interested in being ready for that assessment. After all, we controlled their money.

We noticed a substantial number of programs asking for additional money for security of their IT systems. At first, we did not pay a great deal of attention to this because we were already paying for security in the budget lines of most of the programs that were requesting the additional money. But, they kept coming and were getting more and more urgent. We started looking at the individual program budgets and trying to find out what parts of the budget were actually devoted to security of the systems and it turned out to be harder than we thought. Some programs rolled the money into IT as a whole; some had separate line numbers for these items; some had no reference to anything for security of information systems but included that in their budget for overall security, which included physical, administrative and personnel security matters. It was impossible to separate those relating only to security of computer systems.

By coincidence, the Army was due to present its budget for Information Assurance to the Department of Defense budget process which would vet it, combine it with all the services and agencies in DoD, and forward it up through the federal system. BMDO had to do the same thing, so all the agencies were together for a meeting where these briefings were given. When the Army representative gave his briefing, it included a number of broad security initiatives for all of the major Army networks and several for advanced programs. It sounded pretty good.

Because we were having such a difficult time with understanding how the Army allocated these funds to levels below the senior staff, I asked a couple of questions about how that was done. The responses were confusing, because they weren't pointing to a rollup of funds based on inputs from the field, as the other agencies did, and the Army person was getting flustered. I thought it might be easier for us to understand if we started from the top view and worked down, so I asked him how much of his program was funded as baseline. He said, "None of it." Several of us looked at each other to be sure that we had heard what we thought we heard. He confirmed it by adding that the entire Army program for Information Assurance was an "unfunded requirement" that was submitted as a part of the overall Army budget, but was not included in it for funding. As time went on through the year, the Army would get funds from various places and give them to the IA Office. Incredible as it sounds, the Army still does security of its computer systems the same way today.

We set out to find out where all the money we had been supplying through our budget was going. It was not easy. We matched up what we had given to the Army for missile defense and identified where there were requirements for security included in that funding. The total amount was about $250 million a year. Then, we went to each of the agencies that were supposed to receive the money and figured out how much they actually got to do the work. It was less than half of the money we had given them. At least part of it had been reallocated to expand a military golf course in Atlanta. The rest of it was even harder to figure out and we never did determine where it had gone. The findings put us on a collision course with the deputy undersecretary of defense for acquisitions and the Army chief of staff. General Kadish was caught between his boss in acquisitions and the Army, which did most of the work on his programs, but he didn't do the political thing and forget about it. He had a very simple slogan for all of us: Deliver What You Promise. We liked him because he did.

We decided to try another approach. We were going to include the Army funding for Information Assurance (IA) in our budget and fund it directly to the people doing the work. No middleman. The Army did not like that idea and they thought we could never get this concept through the senior leadership in the Pentagon. Because we were taking a long view, we decided to collect our information and ask for the money in the following year's budget. That gave us about nine months before anyone would know what we were trying to do.

In the meantime, we started asking that every program include a separate line number in their budget for Information Systems Security or Information Assurance. This was so we could track these requests and total them. Most of them began to do that and the numbers rose considerably. They were still not exact, but they were into the $300 million range. BMDO was accustomed to numbers like that, so nobody seemed excited by our totals. When the time finally came, we had a chance to present our budget for the next year and we included any Army system funded by BMDO, and we asked the Army to reduce their budget request by the same amount. Instead of a firestorm, we got a few interested glances but nothing more. Not one person objected.

At the next level up, the budget requests for IA get consolidated and presented as a total. I had never been to a meeting like this and had never been asked to brief such a big group. Most of the time our budget request was so small, it never made the "drop in the bucket" analogy. This time it did.

I got to the meeting early so I could get a seat near the budget director for IA at the far end of a long conference table and wait my turn. As they attendees started to show up, I was surprised to see so many stars on the shoulders of the people sitting with me. The fellow next to me was the surgeon general of the Army and had 3 stars and the one who came with him did too, but I had no idea what he did. By the time they all came in, nobody except me had less than 3 stars. I was pretty sure I was at the wrong meeting. A person in civilian clothes came and sat at the head of the table at the other end and everyone quieted down.

As we went on, it was fairly obvious that they were waiting for something and I figured it was our briefing, but I was wrong. A young colonel got up to brief the budget request of the Defense Information Systems Agency (DISA) and the general next to me turned to his partner and said, "OK, this is it." DISA was asking for 125 people, to be drawn from the other services in the Department of Defense to set up a group to do IA in all of the Defense Department. This confused me, when this was presented, because I had come from that organization ten years before, and had been part of a group of the same size that did the same thing. DISA broke it up and scattered it all over the organization, and now they were asking for another group of people to do the same thing. There were a lot of questions from the floor and I was afraid to say much until all these senior people got finished asking theirs. But I finally got and opportunity and raised my hand. "What happened to the 125 billets you had in the Center for Information Systems Security?" I asked him. Everyone knew, right at that moment, that he didn't have any idea about any such organization, let alone that it came from DISA, and I had to explain it. The chairman asked if the matter could be investigated further before consideration of DISA's budget was made, and the colonel agreed and sat down. The general next to me turned to me and said, "Good job son. We sure didn't want to give up anymore people to those folks."

I was next and gave my briefing. Nobody seemed to care much about it, now that the real issue of the day had been resolved, but the Army representative said he objected to the duplication this could cause and he wanted to be sure we had coordinated this accurately with Army. The Army would agree to establish a separate budget request for IA for the systems missile defense funded, if BMDO would agree to arbitration of their request to make sure there was no duplication of requests. We hadn't expected this but we agreed that this sounded reasonable and we would finish our joint requests in two weeks.

The meetings with the Army office were exhaustive and we went back and forth on the numbers, right up to the deadline. The Army had agreed to a request of over $200 million and we agreed to $7 million. These numbers were fairly equal to what should have been requested in years past, so we agreed. We got the requests to be adjudicated out of cycle and they were passed up the chain for inclusion in the higher-level budgets of both agencies. Everybody left happy at our last meeting.

We thought we had an agreement that would change the way Information Assurance was being done in the Defense Department, but we were not very familiar with the way the Pentagon actually worked. When the Army request got to the next level, it was withdrawn without ever being presented for funding, exactly the same way they had always done it. BMDO was directed to give the Army the $7 million we had requested for Army programs. Once it went to them, it could be used for another addition to that golf course, or anything else the Army wanted it for. It was a very expensive lesson for all of us. Though all the professionals agreed on what to be done, the people at the top of those chains do not necessarily believe that it is important and don't want to change. We can't give the government money and expect anything good to come of it.

The Comprehensive National Cyber Security Initiative (CNCI) is the same, but it is a much more expensive lesson, the amounts of money being classified to protect the innocent. This Bush Administration approach tried to get the government side of the infrastructure working together with our business community. Government leaders have been cited time and time again for weaknesses in security of their systems and there is no mechanism for holding them responsible to the taxpayers for the compromises of information that result. We give money to agencies and expect them to spend it prudently and Congress is supposed to be doing oversight of how that is being done. Congress is clearly sleeping. They are not paying attention to what this money is being used for. But, the sums of money involved are classified; the work they are doing on it is classified; the results are classified, so there is really not much available to talk about in a public forum. We can't make systems secure by throwing money after problems like this when the government leads how it is being spent.

We can't fight a war without straightening up our house first. Getting the infrastructure issues settled should be the first step.

We have columnists on both sides of this saying we already have a Cold War with China, saying it will be too expensive to keep up with and will suck resources from other priorities, those being defined as whatever the right or left wants to say is important. For everyone of these arguments, there were people in wars before us who made them better and more often. We were nearly not in either World War I or II, because so many people were listening to some of them. Nobody likes war and these are good examples of why not, but somewhere along the line we realized that "no war" was not preferable to real war. But, this isn't quite the same thing.

China is not going to stop doing some of the things they are doing now. Economically, they want to continue to grow and expand their influence, taking them into places their military and political structures are not used to operating. Our business leaders cannot find this attractive, but we are not operating on a level playing field. We want them to compete individually with their counterparts in China and the rest of the world, but they are competing with the Chinese government and those counterparts. We have to change our way of doing business.

Second, business leaders have to see more than profitability when it comes to national security. Too many of my friends in government have said that business leaders don't give a damn about the protection of our country. They are clearly wrong about that, but their behavior favors this kind of criticism. Businesses that form alliances with China solely for profit, give up technology to maintain that relationship, and cry about the influence of China on the world stage are hypocrites.

On the flip side of this, all CEOs have someone to work for and profitability is what drives those boards. They can't be gracious and do the work of security in our infrastructure without a clear line to profits. We have to incentivize the people who are responsible for doing it.

In order to do this, we have to put ourselves on a war footing. It needs to be a quiet war that we know about and understand, but we don't tell China anything we are doing. We talk too much, particularly the people in the White House. Perhaps they don't know how to keep a secret, but we are going to have secrets about this war that need to be kept quiet. The Chinese have stepped up their espionage against us, making it harder to keep a secret, even if we know where it is.

It will be a quiet and soft war. We control every aspect of planning and operations for this war and say nothing about it to anyone. It will be a secret, and probably one that we keep better than those nuclear secrets that seem to have gotten away from us. We know how to keep those kind of secrets, when we try. At least we used to.

Those who might be squeamish about even a cold war with China can say, "The Chinese are doing things that look like war to us." We have to believe that these moves of theirs are war-like. No matter what evidence there is, there will always be honest people, public relations firms, and a few governments that will disagree. We should listen, but carefully.

We need to look at what we buy from China and see if there is a way to limit their influence. In the last Cold War, we traded with Russia, but we were careful about it and only for things we thought we couldn't get anywhere else. We just need to think of it the same way. If they want us to give them the capability to make the rope to hang us, we might want to keep that in mind and not give it to them. Once the federal bureaucracy cranks up, there will be no end to what we can do.

We can't do that with the government structure we have now. CIFIUS is too slow to deal with the volume of companies trying to buy into our infrastructure, and a large part comes from overseas acquisitions where we don't have any influence. We needed some international cooperation here. Our industry leaders need to see this as the kind of threat it is, and report any kind of attempt to buy into our systems, especially by China's state-owned companies and front companies. CIFIUS is voluntary reporting.

The federal government has to deal with these seriously and quickly. We have to protect our telecommunications or we are going to get cut off one day. The Chinese are protecting theirs, so it should not be too hard for them to understand why we would want to.

If they are buying up the world's telecommunications, then we need to start helping our businesses compete with that and shut off the sale of anything related to our national networks. When AT&T owned everything, we were better off, in some ways, than we are today. Somewhere along the way, we decided competition was good for the economy and would lower customer prices. It certainly did that, but we forgot about how important that base was to the country as a whole, and sold out our national security for consumer pricing. Our telecoms have to think too much about price and competition and not enough about national security. We need to give them some incentive to think about that more. We should not allow foreign competition — period — even with our friends.

There is quite a bit of spying in a soft-war and we need to increase ours — the human kind, and the kind with electronic gadgets of various sorts. This is the kind of spying that is the CIA. Counter intelligence goes with that, and most of it is the FBI. We don't do enough of either one to even slow down what the Chinese are doing. We should be phasing down military operations to build up the CIA and FBI to handle these types of spying and counter-spying. It will take ten years to build up the types of forces that would be needed to counter the business and government spying that the Chinese are doing, so we don't need to be in a hurry, but we had better get started.

We need to learn from the Chinese. They understand information control and the effect it has on the world. They have done some smart things to control information and keep state secrets. We are far too open with some of those things and could benefit from their understanding, without building our own Golden Shield or intimidating our press corps. Sometimes we equate freedom with being able to say anything. With secrets, that can be harmful.

Last, I think we need a better understanding of war. We don't fight the kinds of wars we used to but we have quite a lot of our people who still think we do. I include many of our senior military leaders and their political friends. We have wasted more money on wars in the Middle East that have accomplished very little and have made our enemies stronger. These kinds of wars have not helped us. We know how to fight an Information War, but we have not been paying attention, while the Chinese actually did it. We can choose to fight now, and ten years later, we may have kept them from completing their objectives. If we wait for the moves of those white stones to be complete, it will be too late.

Chapter Notes

Introduction

1. Carl Von Clausewitz, *On War* (London: Penguin, 1908, 1968).

2. http://abcnews.go.com/blogs/politics/2011/10/obama-sends-100-us-troops-to-uganda-to-combat-lords-resistance-army/.

3. Zalmay Khalilzad and John P. White, *The Changing Role of Information in Warfare* (Santa Monica: RAND, 1999).

4. Shadows in the Cloud, Information Warfare Monitor & Shadowserver Foundation, "Investigating Cyber Espionage 2.0," 6 April 2010.

5. Kim Zetter, "U.S. Considered Hacking Libya's Air Defense to Disable Radar," *Wired*, Threat Level, 17 October 2011, http://www.wired.com/threatlevel/2011/10/us-considered-hacking-libya/.

6. Krebs on Security, "Who Else Was Hit by the RSA Attackers," http://krebsonsecurity.com/2011/10/who-else-was-hit-by-the-rsa-attackers/.

7. "China's First Aircraft Carrier 'starts first sea trials,'" BBC News, 10 August 2011, http://www.bbc.co.uk/news/world-asia-pacific-14470882.

8. http://www.nytimes.com/2009/03/10/washington/10military.html.

9. Eli Lake, "China Bid Blocked Over Spy Worry," *Daily Beast*, 11 October 2011.

10. Criminal Indictment, http://www.justice.gov/usao/iln/pr/chicago/2012/pr0208_01.pdf.

11. Shaun Waterman, "Chinese Firm 'Owns' Telephone System in Iraq," *Washington Times*, 22 February 2011.

12. 2010 Report to Congress of the U.S.–China Economic and Security Review Commission, One Hundred Eleventh Congress, Second Session, November 2010, p. 244.

13. *Capability of the People's Republic of China to Conduct Cyber Warfare and Computer Network Exploitation*, The U.S.–China Economic & Security Review Commission, 9 October 2009.

14. *U.S. National Security and Military/Commercial Concerns with the People's Republic of China*, Select Committee of the U.S. House of Representatives, June 2005.

15. Siobham Gorman, "Electricity Grid in U.S. Penetrated By Spies," *Wall Street Journal*, April 2009.

16. There are several current warnings on counterfeit servers and this is one example: http://www.fujitsu.com/global/services/microelectronics/contact/counterfeit.html.

Chapter 2

1. Bruce Nussbaum, "Stealing Intellectual Property," *Bloomburg Business News*, October 2005, http://www.businessweek.com/innovate/NussbaumOnDesign/archives/2005/10/stealing_intell.html.

2. Johathan Weisman, "U.S. to Share Cautionary Tale of Trade Secret Theft with Chinese Official," *New York Times*, 15 February 2010, p. A-10.

3. Michael Rapoport, "SEC Files Suit Against Third Chinese Company," *Wall Street Journal*, 12 April 2012.

4. James Areddy, Sky Canaves and Shai Oster, "Rio Tinto Arrests Throw Firms Off Balance," *Wall Street Journal*, 13 August 2009 and "China Closes 13 Walmart Stores and Arrests 2 Employees," *USA Today*, http://www.usatoday.com/money/industries/retail/story/2011–10–13/China-Wal-Mart/50751382/1.

5. Lee Levkowitz, Martella McLellan Ross and J.R. Warner, *The 88 Queensway Group: A Case Study in Chinese Investors' Operations in Angola and Beyond*, U.S.–China Economic & Security Review Commission, 10 July 2009.

6. Jamil Anderlini, "China's Security Supreme Caught in Bo Fallout," *Financial Times*, 21 April 2012.

7. Richard McGregor and Kathrin Hillel, "Censors Hobbled by Site Outside Great Firewall, *Financial Times*, 23 April 2012.

8. http://www.france24.com/en/20110811-french-wines-victim-chinese-counterfeiting-chateau-lafite-bordeaux-china-labels.

9. http://www.cbsnews.com/stories/2004/01/26/60II/main595875. shtml.

10. http://www.reuters.com/article/2011/10/11/us-usa-china-lobbying-idUSTRE79A76S20111011.

Products from the People's Republic of China in the Telecommunications Sector, January 2011.

5. Shirley Kan, "China's Military-Owned Businesses," Congressional Research Services, 17 January 2001.

6. See also Mark Weston, *Prophets and Princes: Saudi Arabia from Muhammad to the Present* (Hoboken, NJ: John Wiley & Sons, 2008), p. 281.

7. Robert Herbold, "China vs. America: Which Is the Developing Country?" *Wall Street Journal*, 9 July 2011.

8. http://www.realclearmarkets.com/2011/07/09/in_praise_of_chinese_central_planning_115701.html.

9. James Mulvenon, "To Get Rich Is Unprofessional," Hoover Institute, http://media.hoover.org/sites/default/files/documents/clm6_jm.pdf.

10. America's China Syndrome, posted: 19 August 2003, http://www.wnd.com/?pageId=20358#ixzz1b2qADEoL. See also Jeffrey Lewis, "How Many Chinese Front Companies?" August 2005, http://lewis.armscontrolwonk.com/archive/727/how-many-chinese-front-companies. Lewis says the original number came from the Cox Report in 1999 and, when questioned about it, Cox said "some of the 3000" were front companies.

Chapter 3

1. Dave Lyons, "China's Golden Shield Project," Scribd, Myths, Realities and Context, http://www.scribd.com/doc/15919071/Dave-Lyons-Chinas-Golden-Shield-Project.

2. David Kravets, "Feds Say China's Net Censorship Imposes Barriers to Free Trade," *Wired*, 20 October 2011, http://www.wired.com/threatlevel/2011/10/china-censorship-trade-barrier/.

3. Loretta Chou and Owen Fletcher, "China Looks at Baidu," *Wall Street Journal*, 16 September 2011.

4. U.S.–China Economic & Security Review Commission Staff Report, Nation Security Implications of Investments and

Chapter 4

1. Keith Johnson, "What Kind of Game Is China Playing?" *Wall Street Journal*, 11 June 2011.

2. Joseph Kahn, "Chinese General threatens Use of A-Bombs If U.S. Intrudes," *New York Times*, 15 July 2005.

3. Department of Defense Annual Report to Congress, *Military and Security Developments Involving the People's Republic of China*, 2011.

4. *Capability of the People's Republic of China to Conduct Cyber Warfare and Computer Network Exploitation*, The U.S.–China Economic & Security Review Commission, 9 October 2009.

Chapter 5

1. Steven Levy, "Inside Google's China Misfortune," CNNMoney, 15 April 2011.

2. Shadows in the Cloud, Information Warfare Monitor & Shadowserver Foundation, 6 April 2010.

3. Bill Gertz, "Chinese Spy Who Defected Tells All," *Washington Times*, 19 March 2009, http://www.washingtontimes.com/news/2009/mar/19/exclusive-chinese-spy-who-defected-tells-all/?page=all.

Chapter 6

1. Krebs on Security, "Who Else Was Hit by the RSA Attackers," http://krebsonsecurity.com/2011/10/who-else-was-hit-by-the-rsa-attackers/.

2. Shirley Kan, "China: Suspected Acquisition of U.S. Nuclear Weapon Secrets," Congressional Research Services, February 2006.

3. Carl Meyer, "Are Chinese Spies Getting an Easy Ride?" Embassy, July 2011, http://www.embassymag.ca/page/printpage/spies-07-27-2011.

4. Ibid.

5. *U.S. National Security and Military/Commercial Concerns with the People's Republic of China*, Select Committee of the U.S. House of Representatives, June 2005.

6. In September 2010 the White House released the National Intelligence Program ($53B) and Military Intelligence Program ($27B) numbers for the first time ever.

7. *U.S. National Security and Military/Commercial Concerns with the People's Republic of China*, Select Committee of the U.S. House of Representatives, June 2005.

8. Michael Wines, "China Issues Sharp Rebuke to U.S. Calls for an Investigation on Google Attacks," *New York Times*, 25 January 2010.

9. Reuven Carlyle, "Technology Budget Line Item: $2 billion," http://reuvencarlyle36.com/2010/03/18/.

10. See the declassified report "American Cryptology During the Cold War, 1945–1989" by Thomas R. Johnson, National Security Agency, 1995, p. 87–106, http://www.nsa.gov/public_info/_files/cryptologic_histories/cold_war_i.pdf. COMINT was the category of intelligence collection that NSA was chartered to manage. SIGINT is a subcategory of that and applies mostly to the collection of things that are transmitted between people. These are often encrypted, so cryptoanalysis is included in this charter.

11. Stewart D. Personick and Cynthia A. Patterson, eds., National Research Council of the National Academies, Critical Information Infrastructure Protection and the Law (Washington, D.C.: National Academy of Engineering, National Academies Press, 2003), p. 15, http://www.nap.edu/catalog/10685.html.

12. Kim Zetter, "U.S. Considered Hacking Libya's Air Defense to Disable Radar," *Wired*, Threat Level, 17 October 2011, http://www.wired.com/threatlevel/2011/10/us-considered-hacking-libya/.

13. SiobHan Gorman, "Electricity Grid in U.S. Penetrated by Spies," *Wall Street Journal*, 8 April 2009.

14. Report to Congress, U.S.–China Economic & Security Review Commission, 2010.

15. Von Clausewitz, 102.

16. Phyllis Schlafly, "Buying Counterfeit Chips from China," TownHall, 4 October 2011, http://townhall.com/columnists/phyllisschlafly/2011/10/04/buying_counterfeit_chips_from_china/page/full/.

17. http://www.networkworld.com/news/2006/102306counterfeit.html.

18. *National Security Implications of Investments and Products from the People's Republic of China in the Telecommunications Sector*, U.S.–China Economic & Security Review Commission Staff Report, January 2011.

19. "High Altitude Electromagnetic Pulse (HEMP) and High-Power Microwave Devices: A Threat Assessment,"

21 July 2008, http://www.fas.org/sgp/crs/natsec/RL32544.pdf.

20. Richard Sale, "Stuxnet Loaded by Iran Double Agents," *Industrial Safety and Security Source*, http://www.iss-source.com/stuxnet-loaded-by-iran-double-agents/.

21. Shane Harris, "China's Cyber Militia," *National Journal*, January 31, 2011, http://www.nationaljournal.com/magazine/china-s-cyber-militia-2008 0531.

22. Siobhan Gorman, "President, House GOP Clash Over Cyber Bill," *Wall Street Journal*, 25 April 2012.

Chapter 7

1. Kathrin Hille, "A Show of Force, China's Military," *Financial Times*, 30 September 2011

2. Harry Newton, *Newton's Telecom Dictionary*, (New York: CMP Books, 2001). "The interconnection between telephone company communications and terminal equipment, protective apparatus, or wiring at a subscriber's premises."

Bibliography

Primary Sources

Capability of the People's Republic of China to Conduct Cyber Warfare and Computer Network Exploitation. Prepared by Northrop Grumman Information Systems Sector for the U.S.–China Economic & Security Review Commission. Washington, D.C.: U.S. Government Printing Office, 9 October 2009.

Department of Defense Annual Report to Congress. *Military and Security Developments Involving the People's Republic of China.* (Washington, D.C.: U.S. Government Printing Office, January 2011.

Kan, Shirley. "China: Suspected Acquisition of U.S. Nuclear Weapon Secrets." Congressional Research Services Report RL 30143, February 2006.

_____. "China's Military-Owned Businesses," Congressional Research Services Report 98–197, 17 January 2001.

Levkowitz, Lee, Martella McLellan Ross and J.R. Warner. *The 88 Queensway Group: A Case Study in Chinese Investors' Operations in Angola and Beyond.* U.S.–China Economic & Security Review Commission. Washington, D.C.: U.S. Government Printing Office, 10 July 2009.

National Security Implications of Investments and Products from the People's Republic of China in the Telecommunications Sector. U.S.–China Economic & Security Review Commission Staff Report. Washington, D.C.: U.S. Government Printing Office, January 2011.

Shadows in the Cloud, Information Warfare Monitor & Shadowserver Foundation. "Investigating Cyber Espionage 2.0." 6 April 2010.

2010 Report to Congress of the U.S.–CHINA Economic & Security Review Commission. One Hundred Eleventh Congress, Second Session. Washington, D.C.: U.S. Government Printing Office, November 2010.

U.S. National Security and Military/Commercial Concerns with the People's Republic of China. Select Committee of the U.S. House of Representatives. Washington, D.C.: U.S. Government Printing Office, June 2005.

Secondary Sources

Alberts, David S. *Defensive Information Warfare.* Center for Advanced Concepts and Technology, Institute for National Strategic Studies, National Defense University, Washington, D.C., August 1996.

An Assessment of the Risk to the Security of the Public Network. U.S. Government and National Security Telecommunications Advisory Committee Network Security Information Exchanges, February 2002.

Critical Foundations: Protecting America's Infrastructures. President's Commission on Critical Infrastructure Protection, Washington, D.C., October 1997.

Criminal Indictment, U.S. Department of Justice, Northern District of Illinois, Chicago, http://www.justice.gov/usao/iln/pr/chicago/2012/pr0208_01.pdf.

Gorman, Siobham. "Electricity Grid in U.S. Penetrated By Spies." *Wall Street Journal*, April 8, 2009.

"Information Warfare, Legal, Regulatory, Policy and Organizational Considerations for Assurance." Joint Staff, Defense Department, 4 July 1996.

Khalilzad, Zalmay, and John P. White. *The Changing Role of Information in Warfare.* Santa Monica: RAND 1999.

Krebs, Brian. "*Who Else Was Hit by the RSA Attackers.*" Krebs on Security, http://krebsonsecurity.com/2011/10/who-else-was-hit-by-the-rsa-attackers/.

Libicki, Martin C. *What Is Information Warfare?* Center for Advanced Concepts and Technology, Institute for National Strategic Studies, National Defense University, Washington, D.C., August 1995.

Lyons, Dave. "China's Golden Shield Project, Myths, Realities and Context." http://www.scribd.com/doc/15919071/Dave-Lyons-Chinas-Golden-Shield-Project.

Networks and Netwars: The Future of Terror, Crime, and Militancy. Issue 1362, RAND 2001.

Von Clausewitz, Carl. *On War.* London: Penguin, 1908, 1968.

Waterman, Shaun. "Chinese Firm 'Owns' Telephone System in Iraq," *Washington Times*, 22 February 2011.

Zetter, Kim. "U.S. Considered Hacking Libya's Air Defense to Disable Radar." *Wired*, Threat Level, 17 October 2011, http://www.wired.com/threatlevel/2011/10/us-considered-hacking-libya/.

Index